Effective Parenting and Caregiving

PRACTICAL GUIDELINES FROM PSYCHOLOGICAL SCIENCE

First Edition

E. SCOTT GELLER

Virginia Tech

ANGELA K. FOURNIER

Bemidji State University

cognella®
SAN DIEGO

Bassim Hamadeh, CEO and Publisher
Clare Kennedy, Associate Acquisitions Editor
Tony Paese, Project Editor
Abbey Hastings, Associate Production Editor
Emely Villavicencio, Senior Graphic Designer
Stephanie Kohl, Licensing Associate
Natalie Piccotti, Director of Marketing
Kassie Graves, Vice President of Editorial
Jamie Giganti, Director of Academic Publishing

Cover images: Copyright © 2013 iStockphoto LP/paci77.
　　　　　Copyright © 2018 iStockphoto LP/FG Trade.
　　　　　Copyright © 2019 iStockphoto LP/eli_alsenova.
　　　　　Copyright © 2019 iStockphoto LP/FatCamera.
　　　　　Copyright © 2019 iStockphoto LP/monkeybusinessimages.
　　　　　Copyright © 2019 iStockphoto LP/fizkes.

Printed in the United States of America.

cognella® | ACADEMIC PUBLISHING
3970 Sorrento Valley Blvd., Ste. 500, San Diego, CA 92121

We dedicate this scholarship to family. We appreciate our own parents for their never-ending love and devotion, and for raising us to be passionate about actively caring for others and making a beneficial difference in human welfare and well-being. By the same token, our children have inspired us to continue making a large-scale difference and spreading the Actively Caring for People (AC4P) Movement. This is for you—Krista, Karly, Mia, and Harrison.

CONTENTS

FOREWORD 1

Childhood Experiences Inform My Current Parenting

Krista S. Geller, PhD

"Now don't laugh," I say aloud as I scrunch the corner of a blanket and run it down the nose of my three-month-old. "Don't laugh Harrison!" Right now, Harrison just looks at me and grins. His reaction is not nearly like the reaction I had 40 years ago when my father played that same game with me. "Don't laugh Krista." And before he could say my name I was already hysterical; yet my sister Karly remained stoic and calm, even as Dad ran the ticklish corner of the blanket down her nose.

It is heartwarming and inspirational to note how the concepts, ideas, and loving games we learned from our parents as we were growing up carry into our own parenting styles. I find myself gravitating to my own childhood development and memories—recreating them for Harrison. There are so many memories to choose from; so many adoring thoughts flood my mind when I reflect on my own childhood. I grew up with a pony in my backyard—the wish of many little girls—and the support system of two actively caring parents. Hence, my role models and memories are resilient, positive, and encouraging as I pursue my own path into parenthood.

It is truly inspirational to sit back and reflect on my many childhood memories and personal growth, revealing the most impactful events—both good and bad. But there is nothing like reminiscing childhood memories with a sibling. I often look to my sister Karly as the catalyst, while stitching together recollections from our early years. We create a narrative, combining what we each remember—the details, the reactions, and the behavioral effects of every memory.

Therefore, I begrudgingly say to myself, "Krista, you need to get pregnant again; you must give Harrison a sibling." Nothing compares to a sister or a brother. Karly is my direct reflection; she has been there and has seen it all. In fact, we can both recall every hairstyle we have ever received during our childhood. I can recall many memories she has forgotten or perhaps repressed. We could actually sit and talk for days about our development—what we learned, how we changed, and what we miss the most. It is so very nostalgic to recant our history together and reflect on how so many events directly impacted our lives today, both personally and professionally.

I have marched my feet right next to my father's, or you could say I am traveling in Dad's footsteps. It started at the beginning—when I was born. I am sure my father saw me as an experiment—watching and analyzing my behavior day by day. This was his new past time. Although I did not understand it then, I certainly empathize today with my new son—Harrison. My eagerness to apply my dad's behavioral-science expertise to analyze my son is definitely my new obsession. But back in my early years it was hard to comprehend and grasp Dad's behavioral-science research.

Why was I being asked to participate in all these "weird" experiments? Why was my father having my sister and I "hypnotized"? From one scenario to another, we were followed by data collectors, and later in life I became his data-collection researcher. Each time I did agree to participate, sometimes reluctantly, but in the end I figured I would try my best to learn from the experience. Until age 16, this research experience was baffling and a bit disturbing. What could I learn from this? Today, I see the value of my involvement and use the concepts regularly, but at 16 I didn't get it.

All in all, I was a really good kid; I was not a rule breaker, and I listened to my parents. So, at 16 I had finally earned my driver's license, and it was a new lease on life when Mom threw me the keys to my dad's yellow Jeep and told me to give it a spin. I am telling you, my legs couldn't have carried me faster to the garage for my first drive by myself. But my excitement was drastically halted when I witnessed my dad on his hands and knees dead-bolting a 2-by-3-foot sign to the back of the Jeep. In big bold black letters, it read: "How's my driving, call my dad" with my father's office number printed in red. I stood there stunned, unable to breathe, when Dad spoke up with, "I want to monitor how many people call me with something positive to say about your driving."

At first, I was speechless. Didn't he know I went to high school, a most notorious place for verbal harassment and interpersonal bullying? Didn't he know I would park the Jeep in the school parking lot with everyone else, and parking this vehicle adorned with this sign would be exceptionally embarrassing?

After much debate we compromised, and instead Dad initiated a behavior-based coaching process with me. We first developed a behavioral checklist I would need to use with him every time I drove, and only after receiving a certain safe-driving score would I be granted the privilege to drive by myself. You will read more about this enlightening and informative parent-coaching intervention in Life Lesson 3.

This is just one of the many life lessons my dad provided for me through real-world experience—adding to my growth, inspiring my education, and creating expectations for my continuous learning and development. Although I did not understand nor celebrate many of those life lessons at the time, today I do. I am able to appreciate many concepts and practical applications from those experiences, and I will likely use several on my own developing family. In other words, remembering the direct impact of those "behavioral science experiments" enabled me to better understand myself and my own personal development.

So as you bury your nose in the pages of this teaching/learning manual, and gather theories and intervention techniques for your own actively caring for people (AC4P) parenting, remember this—many of the principles and applications written and explained here were first tested on me.

FOREWORD 2

The Bad/Good Luck of the Draw

Karly S. Geller, PhD

We do not choose our parents and they do not choose us. In that regard, consider the following two true stories that illustrate the bad/good luck of the draw and reveal instructive reality.

Consider Jane. Imagine Jane at 14. She is wearing her grandmother's hand-me-down clothes, constantly wishing her family could afford to buy her the trendy attire her classmates are showing off. Things are not good for her socially. She does well in school to make her parents proud and to be better than everyone else. Unfortunately, her dad was in prison for the majority of her teenage years, and her stepdad died from a drug overdose on her 25th birthday. Although she feels a lack of opportunity and incredible loss, the genuine love in her household is undeniable.

Christmas rolls around just before her 15th birthday. Her mom can finally afford to buy her the in-fashion plaid pants she had wanted so badly. On Christmas morning she couldn't be happier. She put the pants on right away. As she sat down for breakfast, she felt something strange at her feet. To her horror, her baby brother had crawled under the table with scissors and was cutting holes in both legs of her brand-new trousers. This was yet another loss for Jane, but the comfort and sympathy from her mother kept Jane moving forward.

The one reliable person in Jane's life has been her mother. Although it took years for Jane to accept her support, Jane's mother consistently proved her love for her in ways that really counted. She didn't do Jane any favors, but her mom would never leave her out and alone. Some may say Jane's life has been unfortunate. She doesn't have the nicest clothes, but she is the smartest and most creative person you will meet today. Jane's parents shaped her morals, her honesty, her mental toughness, her resiliency, and her patience. She feels privileged.

I am not Jane. My parents are heroes. My dad coached my middle-school baseball team, and my mom taught me strategies required to learn. As a participant in several of my dad's "experiments," I became infatuated with research. When I was three and a half years old, Dad drove me around for hours with a flash card to request adjacent drivers at intersections to "Please Buckle-Up, I Care." More than 30% of those drivers actually buckled up on the spot, and then I flipped over the flash card to reveal, "Thank you for buckling up."

A few unbuckled male drivers actively resisted my behavioral prompt by showing me their middle finger. When I asked Dad what that meant, he replied, "He's telling you you're number one, Honey. He's just using the wrong finger." To this day, the lesson I learned from my father runs deep: The world can be negative, but this only brings you down with your permission. Never let anyone keep you from loving and respecting yourself.

When I was 14, my dad drove my 16-year-old sister and me to 20 different stores surrounding our high school to buy cigarettes illegally. Dad wanted to test the system. My sister and I both wore a wire to record our interactions with each cashier. Out of twenty purchase attempts, I was rejected only once by a cashier who happened to be my basketball coach. And my sister's request to purchase a pack of cigarettes was never rejected.

With this baseline data, my dad went to the local media and obtained front-page coverage. The result: We practically shut down the underage-smoking black market in our town, at least temporarily. Our former popularity in high school never recovered. However, as a current public health professor, I could not be more proud of my participation.

Mom let me pick out my own pony when I was nine years old. She drove me hundreds of miles during my adolescence because I had left my backpack somewhere. During the summer I turned 15, my mom escorted me to seven basketball camps. More recently, my mother accompanied me in her car as I rode a bicycle across the country. I feel guilty when I do not capitalize optimally on the opportunities my parents provided me. My parents shaped my morals, my honesty, my mental toughness, my resiliency, and my patience. I am privileged.

Both Jane and I were raised by parents who loved us immensely. But, the luck of the draw gave me much more favorable circumstances, including a mother and father with the education and professionalism that provided me with so many opportunities to learn and develop optimally. While loving parents want to do the most and be the best for their children, a variety of circumstances hinder or help effective parenting. However, even families with the most favorable circumstances could benefit from this research-based guide on effective parenting.

PREFACE

From birth until forever, parenting never really ends. Sure, our kids grow up, graduate, get a job, get married, move away, and have their own kids. But at any age, your children need you to care for them, to continue to care—to actively care. Parenting is not a passive pursuit. Modeling appropriate behaviors and values, giving instruction and feedback, advice and counsel, are part of the endless arc of parenting, no matter the age of your children. Just think about yourself: Although you are an adult, you might still look toward a parent, guardian, or close relative for guidance and support.

Much of this teaching/learning handbook addresses the actively caring of young children, from infants to toddlers to grade schoolers, and then on to adolescence. And while actively caring is based on love and a range of emotions, it is also effortful work. Effective caregiving is not easy and requires much more than common sense.

This manual targets current and future parents, but it's relevant for professional caregivers: teachers, nannies, coaches, counselors, home healthcare aides, social workers and more. Many caregivers are not professionals; they are older siblings, grandparents, relatives, or even a neighbor who is called on to help with childrearing. You'll notice that we often use the terms "parent" and "caregiver" interchangeably to include readers who are not parents but do actively care for the welfare of a younger person. Although their caretaking might not be 24/7 as it is for a parent, there are many ways to actively care, as we explain throughout the following pages.

You'll also note the emphasis we place throughout the chapters on group discussions, brainstorming, and formal or informal facilitator-led workshops or training sessions. Parenting, of course, is challenging—trying but rewarding. Why do it alone? We encourage you to use this book collaboratively with others (e.g., classmates, friends, relatives) in a series of "book club"–type meetings or study groups. In addition to the average parent or caregiver, this manual and the engagement exercises are ideal for a high school, college, or university course in developmental psychology, human relations, or applied behavioral science. We elaborate on this opportunity later.

After studying, teaching, and researching psychology for more than 50 years, I (ESG) have come to realize the utmost value of seven evidence-based life lessons or human-dynamic principles we all need to practice throughout our daily lives. I've recently authored or coauthored four teaching/learning manuals that detail these psychology essentials for a particular audience: police officers, school personnel, college students, and safety professionals.[1] This guidebook targets parents and other caregivers and is actually the most important of the teaching/learning manuals. Why? Because the content is relevant for almost every human being.

Most people have provided or will provide one-to-one care for a child at some point in their lives—from infancy to adolescence, including perhaps long-distance counseling for an adult son or daughter who questions a career choice, a marriage, or ways to raise their own children.

You may already be a parent or mentor, or plan to care for children someday. Perhaps you work as a nanny or help your family by caring for younger siblings. Beyond your personal life, many careers involve the mentoring of children (e.g., teachers, healthcare professionals, and coaches). The evidence-based principles illustrated in this manual can be applied to each of these situations and make the work of caring for children more effective and enjoyable for both caregiver and child.

If child caregivers were to routinely practice the seven life lessons elucidated in this teaching/learning guidebook, children would be healthier, both physically and psychologically, and everyone would be happier and more successful. Indeed, large-scale application of these principles would improve human welfare in general through enhanced work productivity, environmental sustainability, life satisfaction, and less interpersonal conflict, abuse, and bullying.

Research Foundation

As indicated, the seven life lessons are derived from psychological science and are the bedrock for this teaching/learning manual. They are founded on a strategic integration of applied behavioral science (ABS) and humanism. We call it "humanistic behaviorism" or actively (behavior) caring (humanism) for people (AC4P).

Angela K. Fournier was a star PhD student in clinical science 15 years ago at Virginia Tech, and is currently professor of psychology at Bemidji State University in Bemidji, Minnesota. She has researched and taught ABS, and she has applied humanistic behaviorism in parenting her daughter, Mia, who is currently 13 years old.

Professor Fournier documented some of her effective interventions and the relevant supportive research in a book chapter published by Cambridge University Press.[2] To prepare for that chapter, Dr. Fournier collaborated with another of Scott Geller's former PhD students in clinical science, Kelli England Will, who has been applying humanistic behaviorism throughout the parenting of her daughter, Abigail, and son, Cooper, who are 14 and 12, respectively. Dr. Will documented noteworthy applications of humanistic behaviorism in the book chapter referenced. That chapter was also authored by Dr. Kate Larson, a friend and colleague in parenting and teaching psychological science. Dr. Larson provided information on ABS principles she applies at home with her three children: Lauren, age 10, Samuel, age 8, and Claire, age 6.

Why refer to that collaborative preparation of an academic research-based chapter on effective AC4P parenting? This manual has benefited immensely from the research literature and related applications presented in that book chapter. In fact, many of the parenting examples illustrated in that chapter are reiterated in this manual, but within the context of training an effective AC4P parenting process.

Professor Geller fathered two daughters who both eventually earned a PhD. That was more than thirty years ago, and their mother will testify that Dr. Geller's share of the day-to-day childcare was less than optimal. Yet, it is reassuring that the same ABS principles he attempted to apply many years ago have been applied successfully by the young mothers—Drs. Fournier, Will, and Larson. But 30 years ago the humanistic behaviorism concepts presented here were not documented in an education/training manual.

We are thrilled you have our parenting guidebook. Please read the text, discuss answers to the dialogue-provoking questions, and then practice the lesson-engaging exercises. Your natural or intrinsic reward will be the experience of effective and enjoyable interactions with the children in your care.

ACKNOWLEDGMENTS

His, hers, and ours–writing this manual together has been a most inspirational teaching/learning experience. Each of us has individuals in our lives who have contributed to our *personal* and *professional* accomplishments, and together we acknowledge and appreciate the many people who have contributed to *this* scholarship.

Gratitude from Scott

For more than forty years, I have taught the evidence-based principles and applications of AC4P (or humanistic behaviorism) in workshops and keynote addresses at regional and national professional conferences; and I have documented these in numerous books, manuals, book chapters, magazine columns, and professional research journals. While these presentations might have been effective at teaching the human dynamics of improving human welfare at some level, two limitations have reduced the large-scale ownership and implementation of the research-based information I delivered.

First, many of my presentations (in books, book chapters, and journal articles) have been too academic and detailed to hold the attention of readers looking for practical application strategies. Who has time to wade through a lengthy book that takes up more space describing the theory and research underlying a process than detailing relevant action plans? And second, when specific behavior-change techniques are presented, they often do not fit a reader's particular needs and/or the context in which they are needed.

These limitations have been expressed in evaluations of my presentations at numerous conferences, with statements like, "I appreciate the theory and principles presented by the professor, but I don't know how to apply his teaching at my workplace." Or, "I am impressed with the amount of information presented and the numerous possibilities, but I don't know what to do with all of this. How can I get friends, colleagues, and myself engaged in using this information?"

As a professor of psychology, my coauthor Angela Fournier has similar concerns. She and her colleagues, Drs. Kelli Will and Kate Larson, wrote a brilliant chapter on the behavioral science of childcare for our applied psychology textbook,[2] but this academic scholarship was written for the college/university classroom. By the time most students have an opportunity to apply the parenting strategies introduced and illustrated, the lessons will be long forgotten. Besides, the purpose for reading their informative chapter is certainly not for real-world application, but rather to memorize principles and procedures well enough to answer multiple-choice or discussion questions on an exam. We both realized that we needed to create a teaching/learning manual parents can use in their homes, with opportunities to customize procedures for a variety of applications.

This education/training handbook addresses this legitimate concern in the best way possible. How? By not only explaining the essence of humanistic behaviorism for most effective parenting, but by providing questions, dialogue, and practice exercises to activate the customization of evidence-based AC4P principles for a particular family situation. In other words, this manual instructs and inspires readers to develop and apply effective AC4P strategies for their homes, addressing their distinctive parent/child relationships and concerns.

I want to recognize and thank the many scholars and colleagues who have raised the critical issue of practical application over the years and thereby incited the preparation of this guidebook. These inspirational individuals include the staff of Safety Performance Solutions who have been teaching the AC4P principles and applications covered in this manual to organizations worldwide since 1994. Their queries and insights from the field not only indicated the need for this manual but also influenced its contents.

Many others have inspired the development of this guidebook, verifying the need for a teaching/learning process that enables participants to customize principle-centered AC4P techniques for their culture and provide inspiration and/or guidance. Among these supportive colleagues, a few stand out: Susan Bixler, John Drebinger, Dave Johnson, Bobby Kipper, Nancy Kondas, Tim Ludwig, Steve Roberts, and the late Bob Veazie.

I am also grateful for the creative and instructive illustrations by George Wills of Blacksburg, Virginia; and for the word-processing and text-format support of Jordan Oliver and Kasey Warren. Plus, since 1987 the support system of the Virginia Tech Center for Applied Behavior Systems (CABS) has served as a "think tank" for creating and evaluating innovative approaches to understanding and influencing the human dynamics of interpersonal compassion and intervention, and for developing research procedures to analyze variables that could affect the success of the AC4P Movement. In this regard, I am particularly beholden to my current graduate students: Nick Flannery, Trevin Glasgow, Zachary Mastrich, and Jack Wardale as well as our research scientist, Dr. Erica Feuerbacher.

Thank you all very much, including many supportive colleagues and friends whose names are not listed here. The synergy from your advice and inspiration empowers a laudable legacy: AC4P principles and practices readers can use to enrich their lives and contribute to cultivating a family where AC4P behavior is the social norm and spreads beyond families to the culture in schools, corporations, and the community at large.

Gratitude from Angela

Several special people have substantially influenced my success in the academic and therapy world. Most notable is my coauthor, E. Scott Geller. As a first-generation college student, my academic mentors were more than just professors or advisors; they were special leaders in my life, giving me the guidance and confidence I needed to succeed. Scott has applied the principles in this manual with each of his former and current 54 MS and 39 PhD students, shaping their academic behavior and scholarship with humanistic behaviorism. One of those students—Dr. Thomas Berry—went on to become *my* undergraduate professor and mentor.

I am grateful to Tom for introducing me to psychology, applying the principles outlined here, and leading me to graduate school. I was then fortunate enough to have Scott as my thesis and doctoral mentor, who taught me to apply the humanistic-behaviorism principles through community-based intervention research. I also experienced firsthand the effects of feedforward and feedback; the latter was always more supportive than corrective and given with sincere empathy. Professor Geller's AC4P style of teaching and mentoring were, and continue to be, invaluable in my professional development.

Now I am a university professor, using the AC4P principles to shape my students' research and scholarship. In this academic genealogy, principles of humanistic behaviorism have been passed from one generation to the next. In a sense, this is similar to parenting; whether aware of it or not, as parents we pass on our parenting style—good or bad—to our children. This is why it is so crucial to learn and customize the most effective AC4P parenting strategies.

In addition to my academic mentors, I thank Kelli Will, Elizabeth Letson, and Kate Larson. These women are colleagues *and* mothers who have provided me AC4P guidance and support in *both* areas of my life—personal and professional. Finally, I am eternally grateful to my spouse, Justin. Parenting is challenging work and I could not ask for a better partner.

Gratitude from Scott and Angela

We are both very appreciative of the invaluable collaboration with the Cognella support staff, from Clare Kennedy's initial recognition of the teaching/learning potential of this scholarship to the production vision and leadership of Tony Paese and the creative developmental support of Susana Christie and the invaluable production support of Abbey Hastings. Evidence-based knowledge cannot make a difference without an accepted and appreciated presentation of the information for large-scale dissemination. Thank you Cognella for making this happen.

INTRODUCTION

This manual or guidebook does more than detail practical procedures for effective AC4P parenting and caregiving. It offers research-based principles readers can use to customize their own behavior-improvement techniques for unique individuals and situations, including themselves.

Training versus Education

When we teach a university class, it's considered education, even higher education, but when we teach for industry, the activity is commonly referred to as training. Colleges and universities have centers for educational excellence; industries have training centers. Thus, it seems that colleges and universities educate and industries train.

Is there a meaningful or practical difference between education and training, or can we use these terms interchangeably? Obviously, we do use these terms interchangeably, as if they have the same meaning. But if you think about it, these terms are not the same. Each implicates a different teaching style and a different purpose. Some situations require education, others call for training, and some need both education and training.

Parents and caregivers need to know when to educate, when to train, and when to do both. Let's explore this distinction further. First, let's understand the difference between education and training. Actually, you already know the difference. What do teens receive in public school: sex education or sex training? In contrast, would you have been satisfied as a teenager if you had received only driver education? Are you glad you received some training with that education? As every reader knows and has experienced, the acquisition of any skill—from driving a vehicle, playing a musical instrument, learning a dance routine to participating in a sport activity—requires training of relevant behaviors. Thus, this teaching/learning manual is actually an education/training guidebook.

Misuse of Terms

Because people know intuitively the difference between education and training, misusing these terms can have unfortunate psychological effects. Parenting, for example, can come across as a step-by-step necessary procedure or protocol with no advice or opportunity for individual creativity, ownership, or empowerment. When people are not educated with regard to the principles or rationale behind a particular guideline or recommended practice, they might participate only minimally. They will perceive the program as a requirement rather than an opportunity to make a difference.

By the same token, parental education without follow-up training will not reap optimal benefits. Learning the theory or principles behind an intervention approach is crucial for customizing intervention procedures for a particular individual and situation, but that is not sufficient for nurturing successful parenting and caregiving. Parents need to know precisely what to do in order to carry out an effective intervention. With proper education on validated evidence-based principles, parents and caregivers can refine or upgrade procedures for their diverse circumstances.

Different Techniques

Teaching is different for education versus training. When we lecture to large groups of university students, we use a variety of techniques in an attempt to maintain attention and get participants involved in the learning process. We might use brightly colored PowerPoint slides, show YouTube videos, write extreme statements on a blackboard or flipchart to elicit contrary reaction, or ask pointed questions and solicit answers from the audience.

Our purpose is to influence the students' cognitive or thinking processes. From a practical perspective, we want to expand their ability to improve situations or solve problems related to the subject matter. Such education might increase profound knowledge or critical thinking skills, and this could lead to behavior change. If so, we will have *thought a person into acting differently*. In other words, education targets thought processes directly, and might indirectly influence what people do.

Training targets behavior directly and might indirectly influence thought processes. This typically calls for more than a lecture format, as described for education. Although training might start with a specification of the steps needed to accomplish a particular task, more than that is needed to assure the development of certain skills or procedures.

Participants in a training course should practice the desired behavior and receive pertinent feedback to support what's right, and to correct what's wrong or could be improved. And if such feedback is given appropriately (as detailed later in this manual), behavior might not only be directly improved, but one's thinking or attitude associated with the behavior might be positive and supportive. In this case, training would *act a person into thinking differently*.

This manual provides both education and training. Therefore, the explanation of each research-based principle for AC4P intervention is followed by questions or scenarios to facilitate group discussion. Plus, behavioral exercises are given to practice each principle and receive supportive and corrective feedback for continuous improvement. Your sharing of opinions and ideas with other students, parents, and caregivers will illustrate the variety of relevant applications from one research-based AC4P principle.

Some of these group discussions will become brainstorming sessions of innovative applications for AC4P intervention. And, when some of these possibilities are practiced through interpersonal role-playing with feedback, you will have genuine training that increases the probability of beneficial applications of AC4P principles for most effective parenting and caregiving. While it would be quite beneficial to discuss the principles and explore various applications with groups of parents and/or caregivers, most readers of this manual will not have opportunities to participate in such a discussion group.

AC4P Terminology

At the end of this manual we include a glossary of key terms used throughout the text. The language of psychologists is quite different from that of other professionals (e.g., engineers, physicians, and safety professionals). In fact, behavioral scientists commonly use terminology uncommon in other domains of psychological science. For example, we have coined certain AC4P terms and distinct ways of defining some basic psychological concepts. These terms are bold when first used after this introduction, and defined in the glossary at the end of this teaching/learning manual.

Students with minimal or no background in psychology would find it useful to read this list of terms and definitions before delving into the content. You might want to refer back to this glossary when coming across particular AC4P jargon in the text, or when writing or discussing the answers to questions designed to activate critical parental thinking and action planning relevant to a particular life lesson.

Even if you have had one or more courses in psychology or experienced a workshop on human dynamics, you will benefit from reviewing the glossary. Why? We define each term with a behavioral and/or AC4P focus, and quite often this particular focus results in distinct differences from the more common usage of the term. In other words, we present operational (or observational) and functional definitions through the lens of an applied behavioral scientist.

You might decide to skip the glossary for now and dive into the content of this teaching/learning manual. You will learn evidence-based topical and practical information on applications of humanistic behaviorism to teach and coach your children to be the best they can be. You will come to believe in the need to adopt and promote AC4P behavior among your peers, including children and caregivers, of course. Plus, you will be prepared to teach peers, children, and parents how to cultivate an interdependent AC4P culture of people intervening routinely to benefit the welfare of each other.

An Overview

The first four life lessons reflect the applied behavioral science (ABS) principles of positive reinforcement, observational learning, and behavior-based feedforward and feedback. The subsequent three life lessons are derived from humanism. Thus, the academic label for these evidence-based lessons is humanistic behaviorism. We call it "Actively Caring for People" (AC4P). Here is an overview of these seven life lessons, which are explicated and illustrated throughout this teaching/learning manual for parents and caregivers, as well as your peers who will likely become a parent and/or a caregiver someday.

Life Lesson 1: Employ More Positive Consequences

Applying soon, certain, and positive consequences is the most efficient and effective way to improve both behavior and attitude at the same time. But we seem to live in a "click-it-or-ticket" culture that relies more on negative than positive consequences to manage behavior—from the classroom and workplace to our homes, and when traveling in between. However, human performance is optimized when people approach behavior improvement as success seekers (to gain positive consequences) rather than failure avoiders (to evade negative consequences). It's not enough to understand this life lesson; you need to act on it—hence, the next life lesson.

Life Lesson 2: Benefit from Observational Learning

Observational learning is involved to some degree in almost all human behavior. Consider, for example, how much children learn by watching others—their parents, caregivers, siblings, teachers, peers, and TV actors. The adage "Do as I say, not as I do" does not work. Kids do what they see others doing. And, if the child observes someone receive a positive consequence for a particular behavior, s/he is more likely to perform that behavior. This learning from observation can be facilitated more dramatically if accompanied by behavioral feedback.

Life Lesson 3: Become a Behavior-Based Feedback Coach

The letters of COACH say it all: "C" for care; "O" for observe; "A" for analyze; "C" for communicate; and "H" for help. Start with caring. "Know I care and you'll care what I know. Because I care about your success, I'm willing to observe you and note occurrences of desirable and undesirable behavior."

The observer (parent or caregiver) jots down contextual factors that could be influencing the observed behavior—from situational conditions to potential behavioral consequences. Considering external factors that might influence particular behaviors reflects the analyze phase of behavioral coaching.

Then the observer communicates the information derived from observe and analyze steps. Analogous to humanistic therapy, both behavioral and situational factors are evaluated from the perspective of the person observed, which for very young children is difficult or impossible, of course. The feedback communication is supportive and nondirective. In other words, feedback is not delivered to direct behavior change, but rather to empower personal acceptance and self-motivation for beneficial improvement. We suggest ways to make this happen for children of all ages, even those youngsters who have not yet acquired language skills.

Life Lesson 4: Use More Supportive than Corrective Feedback

Supportive feedback is the most powerful consequence for facilitating a learning process. This training manual details specific guidelines for delivering and receiving supportive feedback. Here's only a brief overview.

For optimal beneficial effect, supportive feedback needs to be accepted and associated with the desired behavior. This happens when the feedback is timely, delivered soon after the target behavior, and meaningful, delivered privately and connected to a noble quality like leadership, integrity, or trustworthiness.

A positive reaction to supportive feedback increases the probability such feedback will be delivered again. Hence, the recipient of supportive feedback (e.g., a child, teenager, or parent) should not deny nor disclaim such acknowledgment with a statement such as "No problem." Rather, listen actively and show gratitude with a smile and a sincere thank you. For preverbal children, a smile, "high five," or a hug may suffice.

Life Lesson 5: Embrace and Practice Empathy

Identifying with another person's feelings, motives, and circumstances is considered empathy, and with empathy comes mutual understanding, appreciation, and acceptance of assignments and/or recommendations for change.

When observing the behavior of a child or adolescent, try and view the situation from that individual's perspective. When listening to excuses for undesirable behavior, see yourself in the same predicament, perhaps reminiscing how you felt when you were much younger and in a similar situation. Imagine the defense mechanisms you might have used to protect your ego or self-esteem. And when considering action plans for improvement, view various alternatives through the eyes of the other person.

Life Lesson 6: Manage Behavior and Lead People

Managers hold people accountable to perform desirable behavior and avoid undesirable behavior. They direct and motivate behavior with an external accountability system. In contrast, leaders inspire people to hold themselves accountable to do the right thing. They facilitate self-motivation by influencing those dispositions or internal person-states that bolster self-motivation. Although managing children's behavior is certainly important early on, as a child matures the need to also inspire self-motivation becomes increasingly critical.

Evidence-based self-determination theory proposes that self-motivation is determined by three person-states: choice (or a perception of autonomy), competence, and community (or a sense of interdependence). Situational and interpersonal factors that influence these person-states are reviewed in this teaching/learning manual, as well as practical ways to enhance them and thereby facilitate self-motivation.

Life Lesson 7: Progress from Self-Actualization to Self-Transcendence

Abraham Maslow's Hierarchy of Needs is a popular theory of human motivation. The assumption: People (even young children) are first motivated to fulfill their physiological needs—the survival requirements of food, water, shelter, and sleep. After meeting these needs, people are motivated to pursue safety and security. Of course, young children learn of these and the later needs in the hierarchy from their parents and caregivers.

Social-acceptance needs are next: the desire to have friends and feel a sense of social support, belongingness, and community. After these needs are achieved, concern shifts to self-esteem: the desire to feel worthwhile, respected, and generally successful. Then, the individual can achieve self-actualization, and at the top sits self-transcendence. At this level people go beyond their self-interests and perform AC4P behavior—from taking time to listen to another person's difficulties, helping a friend or stranger achieve a goal, giving someone supportive or corrective behavioral feedback, or performing behaviors to preserve our environmental resources. While these higher-level needs are essentially irrelevant for young children, the nurturing by parents determines the motivating power of these higher-order needs as the child matures.

Conclusion

The seven evidence-based life lessons from psychological science on which this manual is founded were reviewed in this introduction. Each should be the foundation of any intervention implemented to improve human performance—from childrearing to adulthood and beyond, to the status of "senior citizen." Human welfare and well-being are contingent on the number of individuals practicing these seven life lessons to increase occurrences of AC4P behavior, and inspiring others to do the same. This teaching/learning manual on AC4P parenting and caregiving helps readers translate these life lessons into practical procedures for optimizing the quality of AC4P engagement with others at home, at school, at work, and throughout the community.

Employ More Positive Consequences*

Behavior is motivated by **consequences**. This is the start of our teaching/ learning journey as current or future parents and **caregivers**. Dale Carnegie, author of the seminal book *How to Win Friends and Influence People*, said in 1936 that "every act you have ever performed since the day you were born was performed because you wanted something"[3] We all, parents and children, do what we do for the consequences we expect to get, escape, or avoid by doing it. As Figure 1.1 shows, students' learning is benefitted by realizing explicit consequences.

Of course, young children are also motivated by anticipated consequences following their behavior. Fundamental to the power of positive consequences is the identification of a target behavior to increase in frequency or improve in form. In other words, parents need to define specific behaviors they want their children to perform more or less often.

FIGURE 1.1   Behavior is motivated by consequences.

Identify the Target Behavior

Most of the day-to-day challenges of parenting involve behavior—what you want your child to do,"Eat your vegetables," "Do your homework," or *not* do, "Stop hitting your sister," "Don't run in the house." Still, we often use language with

---

* Portions of this chapter originally appeared in A. K. Fournier, K. England Will, & K. Larson, "Actively caring for our children," in E. S. Geller (Ed.), Applied psychology: Actively caring for people (pp. 469–505). Copyright © 2016 by E. Scott Geller. Reprinted by permission of Cambridge University Press.

our children that addresses a desired internal state or characteristic: "Be nice," "Be good," "Don't be naughty."

Behavioral science informs us that parents are much more effective when they target *observable behaviors*—something a parent can see the child do (or not do). "Be good" is an ambiguous non-behavioral label. It might imply certain desired behaviors (e.g., "Say please and thank you"; "Keep your hands to yourself"), but "Be good" can be interpreted differently by two parents and certainly by children.

If an observable behavior is not specified, neither you nor the child knows whether your expectation has been met. For example, it may be difficult to determine whether your child has followed your order to "Be good," but it's easy to determine whether your child demonstrated good manners by saying "please" and "thank you" at dinner. With young children, more than any other age group, it's critical to identify *specific* behavior that is desired and not desired. And since children don't develop the ability to think abstractly until around age 12, parents should use concrete language when stating expectations and providing **feedback** to young children.[4] Relatedly, it's critical to avoid the use of abstract internal characteristics and the use of negative labels.

Instruct What to Do

Parents should tell children what to do by targeting *desired* behaviors rather than what not to do by targeting *undesired* behaviors. Why? If we tell a child what not to do (e.g., "Don't bounce the ball in the house"), s/he might choose another undesired behavior instead (e.g., throw the ball in the house). On the other hand, if we tell a child what to do, and it addresses the undesired behavior (e.g., "Keep the ball outside"), we can get the behavior we want and avoid a multitude of undesired behaviors. Think of it this way: In any given situation there is probably one behavior we want the child to do and many more behaviors we don't want.

Be clear about desired behavior. This is the best way to get desirable results and is least frustrating for the parent. It's also the easiest way for children to succeed in meeting your expectations. Thus, there's bound to be less negativity from parents. Providing clear expectations reflects AC4P behavior because it sets your children up for success rather than failure. Imagine adopting this **proactive** approach for all aspects of childcare. Later in this life lesson we review Covington's motivational typologies,[5] which promotes the

FIGURE 1.2 Instruct by specifying the desired behavior.

desirable success-seeker **person-state** (i.e., perception, attitude, or disposition) over the undesirable failure-avoider person-state.

Focus on External Factors to Explain Behavior

A toddler's refusal to eat at mealtimes might be attributed to a "picky" palate or a "stubborn" personality. Frequent tantrums in a preschooler might be attributed to a "difficult" temperament. Note the pattern here, problem *behavior* (e.g., food refusal, throwing tantrums), is attributed to internal *characteristics* (e.g., stubborn, difficult). Consistent with the fundamental attribution error,[6] we are likely to attribute the behavior of others, including our children, to internal or dispositional characteristics. Principles of **applied behavioral science (ABS)** advise us to focus instead on external or situational factors—observable things in the environment that can explain a behavioral problem.

Applied behavioral scientists acknowledge the impact of both internal and external variables on behavior. However, ABS focuses on external variables because these can be directly observed and measured, making an objective behavior analysis feasible. External factors are also more controllable, allowing for potential **intervention** and behavior change.

A child's temperament is present from early infancy and is considered by developmental psychologists to be fairly stable.[7] Temperament has a significant influence on behavior, but trying to change temperament is impractical. Even dispositional factors or **person-states** that change more easily (e.g., mood, energy level, perception, and attitude) are inappropriate targets because they cannot be objectively observed and therefore are not easily controlled.

Plus, children, particularly younger ones, can have difficulty identifying and expressing their internal person-states. On the other hand, variables in the child's environment can be clearly observed and in many cases managed to shape healthy, adaptive behavior and influence the occurrence of positive internal person-states.

Let's take the example of temper tantrums. Dispositional causal factors might include hunger, fatigue, or frustration. Observable behaviors may suggest these internal person-states (e.g., a child yawns and rubs her eyes moments before losing it, kicking and screaming in the middle of the grocery store), but we cannot directly observe or control these internal states. However, we can note when and where tantrums are most likely to occur and what seems to happen just before and just after they are observed. Unfortunately, a major temper tantrum is difficult to ignore and often gets immediate attention from a parent.

Depending on the intensity (e.g., the child is screaming loud enough to wake the dead) and location (e.g., in the middle of a crowded store), parents can be quite motivated to stop a temper tantrum immediately. Regrettably, this often means giving children whatever they want. In this and many childcare situations, a parent actually sustains the problem behavior by inadvertently rewarding the undesired behavior. In this case, the parent is experiencing **negative reinforcement**. The probability of the parent's behavior (i.e., giving the child what s/he wants) increases because an undesirable stimulus (e.g., child screaming) is removed. Unfortunately, occurrences of the child's problem behavior increase as the result of **positive reinforcement**. Becoming skilled at identifying and adjusting the antecedents and consequences of problem behavior is crucial for effective parenting.

FIGURE 1.3   A quick-fix solution can lead to a long-term problem.

Be Proactive Rather than Reactive

Proactive childcare is usually more effective and less frustrating than **reactive** childcare for both the parent and the child. In proactive childcare, the parent gives the child a clear behavioral expectation before a possible problem occurs. With reactive parenting, the parent or caregiver waits until a problem occurs and then reacts. Unfortunately, a reactive approach is much more common in our society and typically employs negative rather than positive consequences.

Parents, teachers, coaches, and work supervisors often wait until a problem occurs and then react to it rather than address a potential problem by intervening to prevent the problem. For example, we spend much more money on treating people already sick with *preventable* diseases than on efforts to *prevent* the disease (despite the fact that we could save billions by doing the latter).[8] Childcare is much the same. It seems easier or more convenient to wait until a problem occurs and then react than to think ahead and employ positive consequences to motivate the occurrence of preventive behavior.

Spare the Rod

Would you rather be influenced by positive consequences or negative consequences? Personal experience and common sense give you the answer, and it's been verified by more than 70 years of behavioral research.

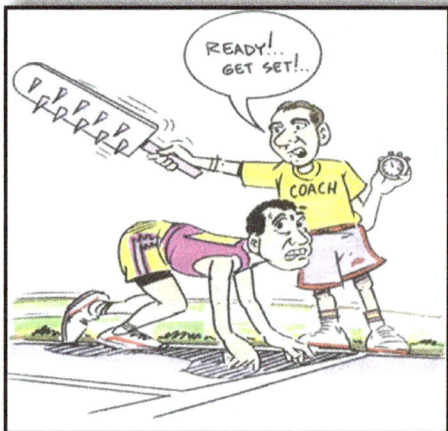

FIGURE 1.4   Working to avoid failure is not fun.

What is your reaction to the illustration in Figure 1.4? Will the athlete run? Of course he will. People react instantly to avoid an impending negative consequence. But how long will the athlete keep running if his coach is not there to hold him accountable? What will his attitude be about running? Will he be self-motivated to run without an **extrinsic accountability system** to keep him going?

For example, "command-and-control" coaching has caused many students to quit a sport. Too many coaches rely exclusively on **corrective feedback** and minimize positive, **supportive feedback** to instruct and motivate athletes. Effective feedback delivery is covered later under Life Lesson 3.

The critical topic of **self-motivation** is covered later in this manual under Life Lesson 6, including ways to enhance self-motivation in ourselves and our children. For now, just consider the potential unpleasant effects of using the threat of a negative consequence to activate **avoidance behavior** and the administration of a negative consequence following the occurrence of an unwanted behavior. "Command-and-control" parenting is common, and as we've explained, usually counterproductive.

FIGURE 1.5   Mandates can be counterproductive.

Furthermore, the top-down negative approach to controlling behavior can lead to **countercontrol**[9] or **psychological reactance**,[10] as depicted in Figure 1.5.

Such contrary behavior occurs when we perceive a restriction or limitation on our freedom or individuality. We act to regain our **personal control**. A child punished for swearing might swear even more when his/her parents aren't around. Others might simply not comply with a rule or regulation when no one's watching.

Yes, it's true that most people do typically follow top-down rules, but usually at minimal levels of compliance. They do only what's required, and no more. For example, a child will read for only 20 minutes after dinner if this is the parental requirement. In contrast, positive approaches to improving behavior can enhance a child's perceptions of personal **choice** or control, as explained in the following life lessons. This can result in even more of the desired behavior than actually called for. With a positive approach, a child is more likely to enjoy reading and read beyond the required minutes in order to progress further in a book they like. Let's look at a negative consequence: spanking children, or corporal **punishment**, as it's sometimes called.

Avoid Spanking

Every family has its own value system and cultural beliefs, which influence the treatment of children. Although the use of corporal punishment is quite common during early childhood,[11] it is not recommended by the American Academy of Pediatrics[12]—for good reason. A spanking might result in compliance initially but noncompliance later. In addition, consistent use of negative consequences can have lasting negative effects on a child. The research on using corporal punishment on children is clear; it's often associated with extremely negative outcomes.

Children subjected to corporal punishment are more likely to show aggression and other conduct problems.[13] They are also at risk for depression, anxiety, and substance abuse.[14] In fact, spanking is not very effective in getting the behavior you desire, and it comes with risks—extra baggage you don't want. When a **penalty** is necessary to address an undesired behavior, the American Academy of Pediatrics recommends using the **timeout** technique, as discussed later under this life lesson.

Discussion Questions

1. Do you recall a spanking episode in your upbringing? How was it implemented and what was the impact on your behavior and attitude?

_____

_____

2. Under what situation(s) or circumstances do you believe some form of corporal punishment might be useful?

_____

_____

3. We all know what happens to our attitude when undesirable behavior is followed by a negative consequence. If we know this, why are negative consequences used more often than positive consequences to improve behavior at home, in school, in sports, in organizations, and throughout communities? Please record your answers to this question here and then participate in a group discussion about various answers, if possible.

_____

_____

A Matter of Mindset

Your answers likely reflect this principle: Behavior-change techniques that are most convenient and rewarded with immediate impact are most popular, at least in the short term. But discuss answers to this question: Which behavior-change technique will have the longest-term benefit? Why?

_____

_____

Often, you can view the same situation as: (a) control by penalizing unwanted behavior or (b) control by rewarding desired behavior. For instance, some of our university students are motivated to avoid failure (i.e., a poor grade), whereas others aspire to achieve success (e.g., a good grade or increased knowledge).

Which students feel more empowered and in control of their grade? Which ones have a better attitude toward class? You know the answers because you've been there. Just think about the difference in your own feelings or attitudes when you perceive your behavior as being influenced by positive versus negative consequences.

Cultivate Success Seeking

Figure 1.6 depicts four distinct achievement-related person-states that have been researched by behavioral scientists to explain differences in attitude and motivation when people work to achieve success versus avoid failure.[5]

A **success seeker** is the most desirable state. These are the resilient optimists who adapt positively to setbacks. Self-confident and willing to take on challenges, success seekers don't evade demanding tasks to avoid failure. They awaken each morning to an *opportunity* clock rather than an *alarm* clock. You can influence this mindset or attitude toward life in yourself and in your children by employing certain situational manipulations and communication strategies, both interpersonal (i.e., with others) and intrapersonal (i.e., self-talk). The beggar in Figure 1.7 has an optimistic mindset—he expects the best.

Failure avoiders do not anticipate success and very much dread failure. By any means necessary they protect themselves from appearing incompetent. They shield themselves from failure by setting the bar low for expectations and applying **defensive pessimism**[15] and/or **self-handicapping**.[16] Young people with this mindset are motivated but "unhappy campers." They say to themselves and others, "I've *got* to go to school; it's a *requirement*," rather than, "I *get* to go to school; it's an *opportunity*."

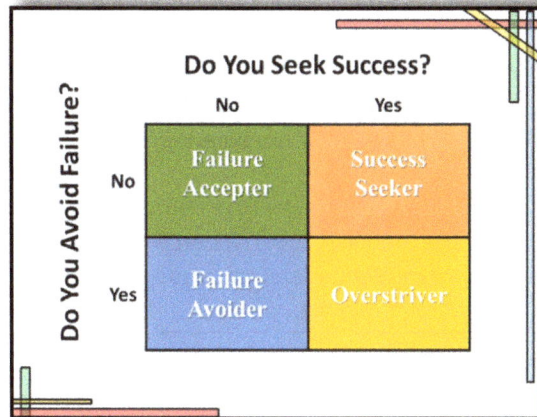

FIGURE 1.6 Motivational typologies defined by achieving success or avoiding failure.

FIGURE 1.7 Optimists experience less distress.

Discussion Questions

1. What conversations do you have with others and within yourself (self-talk) that influence a success-seeking more than a failure-avoiding mindset, and vice versa?

_____

_____

_____

_____

Bottom line: The application of soon, certain, and positive consequences improves behavior and attitude at the same time. Employing this life lesson every day is both critical and challenging. Why? We live in a "click-it-or-ticket" culture that relies on negative consequences to control behavior, from our homes to the classroom and workplace, and during our travels in between. Our government's approach to behavior **management** is to pass a law and enforce it.

2. How does a focus on negative consequences for large-scale behavioral control influence parents, teachers, coaches, school resource officers (SROs), and others responsible for managing the behavior of young children, adolescents, and teenagers?

_____

_____

Spoil the Child

On the other end of the consequence continuum, some complain that American society has gotten too soft and children are rewarded too often. Every child receives a "participation ribbon." Some suggest that constantly rewarding or praising children for their behavior decreases self-motivation, robbing them of the feeling of success or true accomplishment. Alfie Kohn, author of the book *Punished by Rewards,* suggests rewarding behavior is a form of control that decreases internal or self-motivation and makes one dependent on extrinsic **rewards**.[17] Regarding parenting, he claims praise, medals, ribbons, and trophies, as well as other positive consequences for desirable behavior, are gentle forms of coercion that teach children to focus on what others think of their behavior rather than on what they think and feel about themselves.[18]

Praising Ability vs. Effort

So, are rewards good or bad? Substantial research suggests the answer depends on certain circumstances, but Kohn is much more wrong than right. Let's refer to Carol Dweck's research on children praised for either their ability or their effort. Carol Dweck, a noted scholar in educational psychology, has argued convincingly that praise can actually undermine children's skill development if given the wrong way.[19] She recommends that praise for children and adolescents should be certainly given, but such praise should be linked directly to children's work effort and task mastery (**process-oriented feedback**) rather than to their abilities. And just showing up for an opportunity to participate in a worthwhile event is not enough. It's the behavioral effort that earns the reward.

Supportive Research

Dr. Dweck and her colleagues gave hundreds of early adolescents a set of 10 fairly difficult problems from the nonverbal portion of an IQ test. Afterward, all participants were praised individually for their performance on the test, but the nature of the praise was varied systematically. For half of the students, the praise was based on their *ability*. Each child was told, "Wow, you got eight right. That's a really good score. You must be smart at this" (p. 71).[20] The other students were each praised with a positive social label for their *effort* with these words: "Wow, you got eight right. That's a really good score. You must have worked really hard" (p. 73).[21]

Both groups scored equivalently on the IQ test. But researchers noted significant differences in students' behavior following their **ability label** versus **effort label**. All students had the choice to work on a challenging new task from which they could learn. Most of those with the ability label rejected this opportunity. Apparently "they didn't want to do anything that could expose their flaws and call into question their talent" (p. 72).[21] In contrast, 90% of the students praised for their effort welcomed the opportunity to take on a challenging new task from which they could learn.

Later, when *all* of these students performed less effectively on some additional, more difficult problems, their reaction to failure was influenced by the prior label given them. The ability kids felt like failures. They believed they did not live up to their ability, and they rated the task as "not fun anymore." In contrast, the effort group saw in their failure a need to try harder. They did not perceive any indictment of their intellect and did not indicate they didn't enjoy the new problem-solving task. Many of them said that the hard problems were the most fun.[21]

After experiencing these difficult problems, the adolescents were given some easier problems to solve. The performance of the ability-labeled students plummeted. The effort-labeled students performed increasing more effectively. In the profound words of Dr. Dweck, "Since this was a kind of IQ test, you might say that praising ability lowered the students' IQs. And that praising their effort raised them" (p. 73).[22]

A final difference showed up when the adolescents were asked to write out their opinions of the problem-solving tasks for the benefit of students at other schools. A space was provided on this form for the students to report the personal scores they had received. To the researchers' surprise and disappointment, 40% of the ability-labeled students reported higher grades than they actually earned. In the author's words, "We took ordinary children and made them into liars by telling them they were smart."[22]

A Coaching Example

Suzie is a 6-year-old child who has recently joined a gymnastics program. In one of the practice sessions, Suzie and her teammates are learning to do cartwheels. It's Suzie's turn to perform, and she does a very good cartwheel. Rightfully so, her coach wants to reward her performance. She gives Suzie ability-oriented feedback with the comment, "Suzie, that was so good. You are a born gymnast!" This coach has given Suzie an *ability* label, attributing her good performance to something innate or inborn.

In contrast, an *effort* label is reflected by the comment, "Suzie that was so good. You have worked really hard the last few days to learn how to keep your elbows locked and your legs straight. And now look what you can do!" As you know, this effort label is more effective, because it helps Suzie develop the mindset that her effortful behavior

FIGURE 1-8   Reward effort, not ability.

led to the successful outcome and she can control her performance outcomes and improve.[19] The ability-oriented feedback (although nice to hear) does not give Suzie a perception of control over her success.

If Suzie's coach continues to provide ability-oriented feedback (e.g., "You are a natural athlete"), when Suzie encounters a skill she initially cannot do (e.g., a more complicated gymnastics skill), her mindset may be that she does not possess the innate ability to develop that particular skill set. Plus, she might not attempt more difficult routines because she fears losing her positive ability label.

On the other hand, if Suzie's coach were to consistently give her effort-based praise (e.g., "When you perform a skill really well, it's because you have worked hard to master it"), then when Suzie encounters a difficult routine she initially cannot do, she will have a growth mindset (i.e., "I can't do that routine now, but if I practice really hard, I will learn to do it").

Bottom line: This research provides solid evidence for the ABS principle of focusing on behavior rather than an internal person-state. Plus, when a child's behavior (demonstrating effort) is praised, both performance and related person-states improve. And if the verbal behavior associated with the delivery of a reward facilitates a child's perception of competency, choice, and/or social support, self-motivation is activated. This increases the probability of behavioral sustainability.

Praise Junkies

Another concern regarding the use of praise is that children may become "praise junkies,"[17] requiring more and more recognition for even the most basic behavior. To the contrary, the research literature consistently refutes concerns of over-rewarding children's behavior and overwhelmingly supports the efficacy of using positive consequences to reward the behavior or effort of children.[23] However, this does bring up an important caveat: ABS strategies are implemented to facilitate *learning*—a relatively permanent change in behavior.

The mission of parents is to help children learn appropriate behavior in various situations. This often means using positive consequences to increase the frequency or improve the quality of a desired behavior. Once a behavior has been learned and is performed consistently, the delivery of extrinsic consequences should be decreased over time.[24]

The Premack Principle

Grandma said, "If you eat your spinach (or whatever food you didn't like but was good for you), then you may have dessert." This reflects a seemingly commonsense idea: Allow opportunities to do pleasant activities after less pleasant but desired behavior is performed first.

David Premack developed and researched this unique and practical approach to **contingency management**: setting up an **incentive**/reward process to motivate the occurrence of desirable behavior.[25] Instead of defining positive consequences or a reward in terms of stimuli or events (e.g., candy, money, trophy, or an award ceremony), he defined rewards as the opportunity to do something desirable. It's not the candy but the opportunity to eat the candy; it's not money per se, but the behavioral opportunities money can buy—the privilege to purchase goods and services, attend entertaining events, and enjoy safe environmental settings.

Though much of his research involved chimpanzees and monkeys, Premack tested this principle with young children (average age was 6.7 years). In his seminal study, a non-preferred activity had to be completed in order to get access to a preferred activity. Preferred activities included playing pinball or eating candy, where the activity preferred by each child was established by observing him/her in a **baseline** phase. During baseline, children rarely did a non-preferred activity if allowed free access to their preferred activity.

During the intervention phase, the less-preferred activity had to be performed in order to gain access to a preferred activity. The children usually had to be told how one behavior led to the other, but once the connection was made, the children did the less preferred activity in order to gain access to the preferred activity.

How do you determine what activities people prefer? Careful observation is critical. You may notice a child play a video game continuously if left to his/her own choices. You may notice room-cleaning happens infrequently, if ever. To get a child to increase the occurrence of room-cleaning behavior, withhold access to video games until the room is clean. Another child may not like to play video games but may spend a lot of time listening to music, playing with toys, reading comic books, watching TV, or surfing the Internet. Behavior that occurs spontaneously at a high rate can be used to reinforce behavior that happens less often.

Students use the **Premack Principle** when they require themselves to study a certain amount of time before engaging in a more pleasant activity like watching TV, texting friends, browsing the Internet, or playing video games. This is self-management with the Premack Principle.

Teachers use the Premack Principle when they promise their students extra recess after they complete certain classroom learning exercises. So, if you want your child to perform a behavior s/he does not like to do, offer him/her the opportunity to perform a behavior s/he likes to perform after s/he completes the less pleasant task or chore: "You may go out and play with your friends after you complete your daily chores."

Discussion Questions

1. How often did your parents use a positive consequence to reward desirable behavior?

_____

_____

_____

2. Please describe a **reward contingency** used to influence your childhood behavior.

_____

_____

_____

3. What impact, if any, did the reward technique from Question 2 have on your behavior, feelings, and motivation?

_____

_____

_____

4. Did you ever feel over-rewarded for performing desirable behavior? If so, was your self-motivation hindered?

_____

_____

_____

5. Describe how you could use the Premack Principle to manage your own behavior.

_____

_____

_____

6. Explain an application of the Premack Principle to increase the frequency of a desirable behavior of a child under your care who does not like performing that behavior.

_____

_____

_____

The Reward Chart

A reward chart like the one shown in Figure 1.9 can be quite effective for addressing most behavioral issues. Note that the focus on the chart is achievement: *doing* desired behaviors, not *stopping* undesired behavior. Reward charts put Life Lesson 1 into action and can be useful for children after age 3 and can be used throughout life. Indeed, many adults track their own behaviors or desirable effort on a chart (e.g., recording daily calories consumed, exercise behaviors, projects completed), and they use the results for self-management and self-motivation. By age 3 most children can make performance-related judgments and thus should be able to understand the concept of earning a sticker on a chart for performing a desired behavior.[26]

It's futile to use a reward chart before a child can understand an **if-then reward** contingency. The child needs to make the connection between the desired behavior and the positive consequence.

Mia's Reward Chart

Job	S	M	T	W	T	F	S
Pick up Toys							
Brush Teeth							
Make Bed							
Do Homework							
Extra							

FIGURE 1.9   Reward chart for a 7-year-old girl.

When it's easily visible to the child, the chart serves as an activator (Lesson 3), reminding the child of the desired behavior and the positive consequence(s) of performing the behavior.

The chart in Figure 1.9 was used with a 7-year-old girl. The goal was to increase several daily behaviors regarding schoolwork and self-care. Although her parents defined the desired behaviors, referred to as "jobs," the child was involved in negotiating the rewards, writing the rewards on the chart, and deciding where to keep the chart (see Figure 1.10). Involving the child gave her ownership in the process and increased her motivation to do the tasks and earn the rewards.

Note the "Extra" row in the "Job" column. In the true spirit of self-motivation (Lesson 6) this allowed the child to be rewarded for going above and beyond the required daily tasks (e.g., helping parents, caring for pets) and experience a sense of **competence**, choice, and connection to others.

The child earned a sticker to place on the chart after completing a chore. This served as an *immediate* positive consequence. After earning a designated number of stickers, the child was rewarded with a larger prize, such as a chance to go on a special outing. This was a *significant* positive consequence.

Parents can make their own personalized reward charts or download charts available online. Several websites (e.g., kiddycharts. com) provide reward charts that can be downloaded and printed at no cost. For the child who loves mobile games and applications, free mobile apps are available (e.g., Chore Monster) for maintaining engagement and helping both the parent and child track behaviors and opportunities to provide a rewarding consequence.

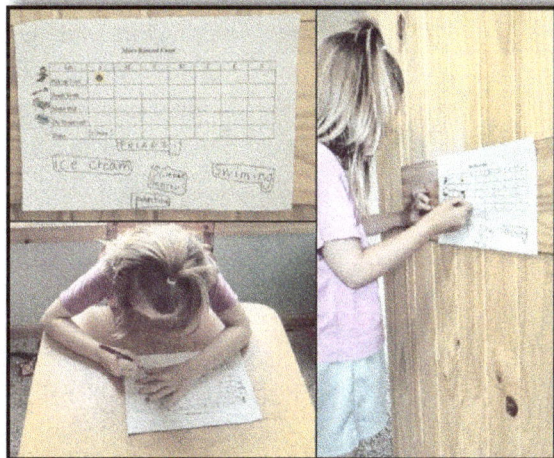

FIGURE 1.10   Establishing ownership in a reward chart: a reward chart printed from a home computer (upper left); the child writes potential prizes to be earned (lower left) and puts stickers on the chart for doing the desired behavior (right).

Discussion Exercise

1. Create a potential reward chart for a child in your life. How would you involve the child in designing and implementing this application of positive consequences to motivate desirable behavior?

_____

_____

The Timeout Process

Consistent and frequent use of positive consequences is best for increasing the occurrence of desired behavior, but other techniques are sometimes necessary to decrease the frequency of undesired behavior. Ignoring minor infractions and providing redirection can work wonders with small children, but these are inappropriate for more serious misbehavior.

Timeout, when used correctly, is a very effective technique for managing a child's misbehavior. It's a recommended alternative to spanking, which, as discussed earlier, has serious and potentially long-lasting negative effects on children's conduct and mental health and can increase interpersonal aggression and bullying behavior.[27] And along with all these negative side effects, spanking only suppresses unwanted behavior temporarily.

It's surprising that an adult's emotional reaction to undesired behavior can actually reinforce such behavior. Indeed, attention of any kind can be rewarding for some children, and thus while the parent is busy cooking dinner, a child misbehaves for parental attention. Timeout avoids this problem and also avoids a common pitfall for many parents: empty threats without a negative consequence (e.g., "Keep doing that and you will not go with us on the family vacation."). Timeout is easy to apply directly, consistently, and immediately, and without **emotion**.

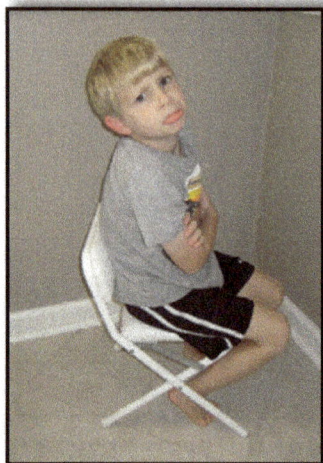

FIGURE 1.11 A child in timeout, appropriately removed from stimulation.

"Timeout" is short for "timeout from positive consequences." Its purposeful removal of attention—good or bad—is the negative consequence for the child. Timeout occurs for a distinct span of time without stimulation, without parental or other attention, and without fun or any distracting activity. When done correctly, it's an unpleasant but passive experience. The general guidelines for implementing an effective timeout procedure are as follows:[28]

1. The caregiver makes some decisions in advance, including the length of time for timeout and the typical timeout location. A chair, stool, or spot on the floor that is removed from stimulation but can still be monitored by the caregiver is best (see Figure 1.11). In a pinch, any spot that is relatively devoid of stimulation can serve as a place for timeout. The recommended minimum length of timeout is 1 minute for every year of the child's age.

2. When misbehavior warrants a timeout, the caregiver first gives the child a warning. This involves making a command (not a request, but a command) in a businesslike but pleasant demeanor and tone of voice.

3. The caregiver waits for about 5 seconds. If the child does not comply (or if the unwanted behavior recurs in a short period of time), the child is immediately told to go sit in the timeout chair/spot. It may be necessary for the caregiver to lead him/her by the wrist to the timeout chair.

4. The caregiver tells the child to stay in the chair until s/he says it's okay to come out. It's helpful to set the stage for achieving success by telling the child s/he must be quiet and stay in the chair before earning the right to leave timeout.

5. The caregiver goes about his/her business while the timeout is served, keeping an eye on the child's behavior. The caregiver does not interact, argue, or otherwise engage with the child. The key is to seemingly ignore the child while unobtrusively monitoring his/her behavior and watching a clock. Some caregivers use a timer, which is okay provided the caregiver determines when the child can leave timeout and does not rely solely on the timer alarm for this determination.

6. The child can leave timeout when three conditions are met: (a) the minimum 1-minute-per-year-of-age sentence is served; (b) the child is no longer kicking/screaming/throwing a tantrum and is quiet for a few moments; and (c) the child agrees to comply with the original command or correct the action that got him/her in timeout (e.g., in cases of hitting a sibling, the child apologizes and agrees not to do it again).

7. To end timeout, the caregiver asks the child in a calm voice to explain why s/he received a timeout. It's important for the child to understand the behavior that led to the timeout and to immediately perform the necessary action to correct the inappropriate behavior. It's beneficial for the caregiver to reassure the child of his/her love and to comfort the child after a successfully-served timeout.

It's amazing how often parents make mistakes when applying the timeout technique. The result: Timeout doesn't work because its hallmark purpose—removal of positive consequences—is spoiled when the technique is used incorrectly or inconsistently.

Here are 10 common ways caregivers use timeout *incorrectly*:

1. Multiple warnings are given, or no warning is given before timeout. (With the exception of particularly egregious behaviors such as hitting another child, *one* warning command should be given.)

2. Timeout is delayed to a later time.

3. The caregiver places the child in a timeout location that is interesting (e.g., in front of a window, in view of the TV, in the proximity of other children, with a

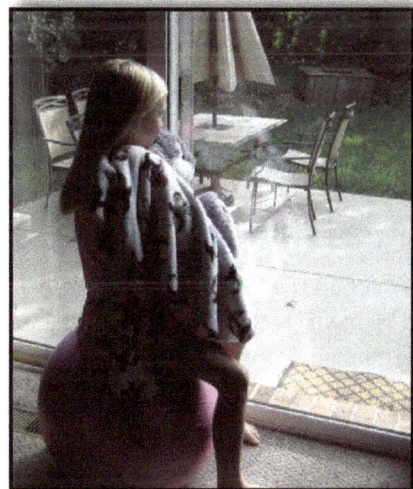

FIGURE 1.12 An ineffective timeout location; the child is in a stimulating environment with a comfort toy/object.

book), or the child is allowed to have a comforting toy or blanket. Figure 1.12 shows a poor timeout location.

4. The child is sent to his/her room (or another room) unmonitored during timeout, or the timeout setting is a scary or unsafe place (e.g., closet, dark room, bathroom).
5. The caregiver or others interact with, talk to, argue with, or negotiate with the child during timeout.
6. The caregiver stares at the child rather than doing something else during the child's timeout.
7. The child is allowed to leave the location during the timeout period.
8. Timeout is too short or too long.
9. The child is permitted to leave timeout when the time is up regardless of his/her behavior during timeout, such as throwing a tantrum or yelling at a parent.
10. The parent fails to talk with the child in a calm and comforting manner immediately after the timeout to ensure the child understands what behavior led to the timeout; or the child is not required to correct or amend the inappropriate behavior after the timeout period (e.g., apologize for misbehavior, do the chore the child had refused to do).

Timeout applies key ABS principles, and when it is used correctly, the undesired behavior is quickly extinguished. Timeout also deescalates situations that could otherwise result in an emotionally charged parent-child interaction. For additional guidance in dealing with undesired behavior and *what-if* scenarios, Russell Barkley's *Your Defiant Child*[29] and *Defiant Children*[30] are useful evidence-based resources for parents and clinicians, respectively.

Discussion Questions

1. Have you ever experienced a timeout procedure as either the deliverer or the receiver? Please explain the process and its impact on behavior and attitude.

_____

_____

_____

_____

2. "Grounding" or removing social interaction privileges for a specified time period is a common "punishment" technique experienced by adolescents and teenagers. How is this technique related to the timeout process?

_____

_____

_____

_____

Benefit from Observational Learning

2

If you want to be better at what you do, watch someone who performs that task better than you. Yes, parents could improve their parenting by observing the child-caring behaviors of successful parents. The power of **observational learning** is obvious; a large body of psychological research indicates this type of learning is part of almost everything we do.[31]

Our actions influence others more than we realize. Children learn by watching us at home; colleagues are influenced by our actions at work. We're often unaware that we wield this influence. What might children learn by watching the driving behavior of their parents, including their parent's verbal behavior? Figure 2.1 shows how parents may not realize how much their behavior shapes their children's actions.

As adults, we teach others, especially children, by example. As the figures in this chapter show, children learn new behavior patterns, including verbal behaviors, by watching and listening to their parents. In this way, they learn what is expected of them in various situations.

Our actions influence others to a greater extent than we realize. Not only does the occurrence of risky behavior (e.g., not using protective safety gear like a bike helmet or vehicle safety belt) encourage similar behavior by observers, but verbal behavior can also be influential. If a caregiver is observed commending a child for AC4P behavior or reprimanding someone for bothersome behavior, observers may increase their

FIGURE 2.1 We learn much from observation.

"WHY DON'T YOU HAVE TO WEAR A HELMET, MOM?"

FIGURE 2.2 Parents need to set the right example.

FIGURE 2.3 Observational learning is not always sufficient.

performance of similar behaviors (through **vicarious reinforcement**) or decrease the frequency of similar undesirable behavior (through **vicarious punishment**).

Bottom line: To develop desirable behavior as the norm—rather than the exception—we need to set a good example both in our own practices and in the verbal behavior we offer others. In other words, you never know when you're being observed. If you believe in the lessons you're teaching children, it's important to walk the talk. The power of observational learning is illustrated by the poem below by Forrest H. Kirkpatrick.

The eye's a better teacher and more willing than the ear;

Fine counsel is confusing, but example's always clear;

And the best of all the preachers are the ones who live their creeds.

For to see the good in action is what everybody needs.

I can soon learn how to do it if you'll let me see it done;

I can watch your hands in action, but your tongue too fast may run;

And the lectures you deliver may be very wise and true.

But I'd rather get my lesson by watching what you do.

Figure 2.3 provides a memorable pictorial regarding the influence of observational learning on behavior.

Discussion Questions

1. Recalling your childhood, what desirable behaviors (e.g., table manners, safety-related behaviors, household support, food choices and/or preparation) did you learn by watching the behavior of your parents or caregivers?

_____

_____

_____

_____

2. Recalling your childhood, what undesirable behaviors (e.g., inappropriate language, verbal abuse, inter-personal aggression, alcohol consumption) did you learn by watching the behavior of others?

_____

_____

_____

_____

3. To what extent do you believe the media (e.g., TV, movies, YouTube, Snapchat, Instagram, Facebook, Twitter) set desirable versus undesirable examples for our children?

_____

_____

_____

_____

4. List some TV shows, movies, or other media that could have a desirable behavioral impact on viewers of certain ages. In other words, what current media presentations promote desirable behavior among young children, adolescents, and teenagers? Consider verbal behavior in your answers.

_____

_____

_____

_____

5. What particular TV shows, movies, or other media are likely to have an undesirable behavioral impact on viewers of certain ages? In other words, list current media presentations children of certain ages should not be permitted to watch. Why did you select each of these productions for the selected age range?

_____

_____

_____

_____

_____

Improve with Behavioral Feedforward and Feedback*

3

"Practice makes perfect" is simply not true. Practice makes permanence. Behavior improves only through the repetition of behavior-focused feedback. Sometimes feedback is a natural consequence—the young girl sees where her basketball lands after shooting at the basket. But even when we observe an outcome of our behavior, behavioral feedback from an observer (e.g., a coach) is needed to properly adjust and improve our performance.

People of all ages, including children and adolescents, want to be competent at skills they believe are meaningful or worthwhile. So, how can they become more competent at worthwhile tasks? You know the answer: relevant behavior-focused feedback. But who should deliver improvement feedback? Adults (e.g., parents, teachers, coaches, and police officers) need to give children and adolescents supportive and corrective feedback. Plus, they need to give each other behavioral feedback about their delivery of behavioral feedback. The letters of COACH capture it all: C for care; O for observe; A for analyze; C for communicate; and H for help, as depicted in Figure 3.1.

Caring kicks off the coaching process. Caring cannot be emphasized enough in the context of parenting and caregiving. Think about the term "care-giving." That says it all. "Know I *care* and you'll care what I know. I care so much, I'm willing to *observe* you and notice the occurrences of desirable (or effective); and undesirable (or ineffective) behavior." It's critical to note environmental factors

---

*   Portions of this chapter originally appeared in A. K. Fournier, K. England Will, & K. Larson, "Actively caring for our children," in E. S. Geller (Ed.), Applied psychology: Actively caring for people (pp. 469–505). Copyright © 2016 by E. Scott Geller. Reprinted by permission of Cambridge University Press.

Care
- show that you care
- set caring examples

Observe
- define target behaviors
- record behavioral occurrences

Analyze
- identify existing contingencies
- identify potential contingencies

Communicate
- listen actively with empathy
- take a nondirective stance

Help
- recognize continuous improvement
- teach and encourage the process

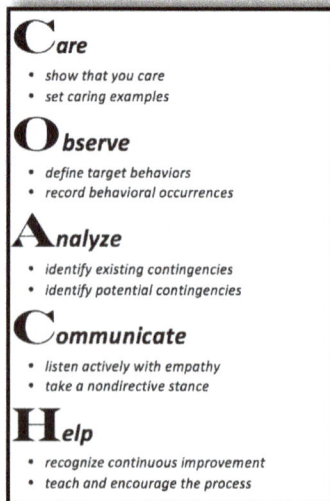

FIGURE 3.1 The five basic components of AC4P coaching.

that may influence observed behavior, from household conditions (e.g., distracting noise) to behavioral consequences (e.g., rewards). This is the *analyze* phase of coaching.

Interpersonal *communication* comes next. How should you deliver information gained from your prior observe and analyze steps? Although everyone wants to improve, many resist giving and receiving the kind of communication critical for positive behavior change. Again, we can't emphasize enough the critical importance of effective communication in the context of parenting and caregiving. You cannot provide care or achieve the behaviors you desire as a parent without giving children—and yes, receiving from them—behavior-focused feedback.

To overcome resistance to behavioral feedback, effective behavior-improvement coaches steer clear of providing overwhelming advice at once. Don't suddenly ask your child to change his/her entire routine for completing school homework. Instead, emphasize incremental fine tuning or successive approximations and accentuate the positive—occurrences of desirable behavior—to facilitate behavioral and attitudinal improvement. "That's great; now organize your math homework like you did for your social studies homework."

Help, the last letter of COACH, is accomplished if the interpersonal communication goes well. The behavioral feedback is accepted and used to improve the pinpointed behavior. Note how the four letters of help—*humor*, *esteem*, *listen*, and *praise*—reflect strategies that increase the probability that your advice, directions, or feedback will be appreciated and accepted. Children are more likely to accept feedback from parents who deliver it with some humor, and in a way that promotes **self-esteem**, through active listening and appropriate behavior-based praise. And it goes without saying that *helping* is an essential "core competency" of the parenting or caregiving of children.

The Misuse of Feedback

Imagine your child receives a request from a teacher to stay after class to receive some "feedback." Or, you inform your child that you would like to have a private discussion in order to offer some feedback. How would you feel if you were on the receiving end of these feedback requests? Would you envision these interactions to be unpleasant with negative emotions? Would your child expect a positive interaction when his/her teacher or you announce the need for a feedback discussion? How relevant is Figure 3.2?

FIGURE 3.2 Feedback often implies a negative consequence.

Two common characteristics of feedback influence people's desire to avoid feedback and justify the negative reaction. First, negative or *corrective* feedback typically takes precedence over positive or *supportive* feedback. Most of us, including children at home, in school, with friends, or participating in sports, experience this unfortunate tendency almost daily.

Bottom line: Many parents, teachers, coaches, and supervisors in work situations use reprimanding more often than praise, with the apparent belief we learn more from our mistakes than our successes. Empirical research and even common sense indicate the fallacy of this apparent belief.[32]

The second reason feedback carries negative baggage is that we often correct others—including our children—without focusing solely on their behavior. The way feedback is delivered suggests the problem or error observed extends beyond behavior. "You're lazy." "What a careless thing to do. What were you thinking?"

It's much easier to influence behavior than a person-state. For example, telling a child you're dis-

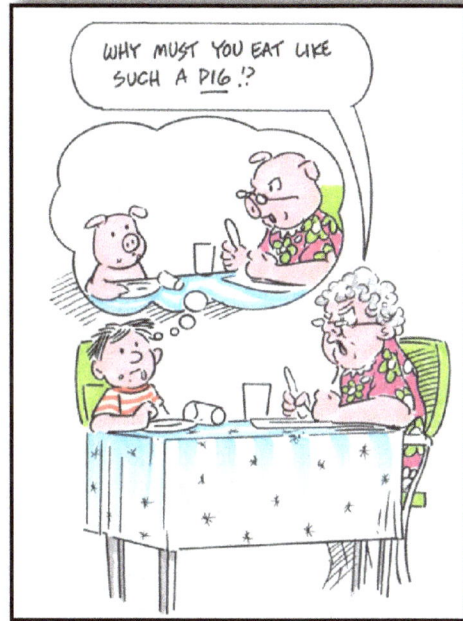

FIGURE 3.3 Nonbehavioral labels can be misleading.

appointed s/he didn't clean her/his room is much less threatening to the child's sense of self than telling the child s/he is "sloppy" or "messy." *Sloppy* and *messy* are labels, suggesting the problem is global and permanent—a part of who they are. Using ability labels in this way can contribute to a negative self-concept, with children identifying themselves as "bad," "rude," or "sloppy."[19] Remember, a child or a teenager's sense of "self" can be fragile and vulnerable, and it is always evolving.

People tend to live up to the labels they are given, whether the label is positive or negative, according to the research of Dweck[19] and Kraut.[33] This is true for both young children and adolescents. Children labeled "neat and tidy" are more likely to clean up after others, and children labeled "delinquent" tend to engage in further delinquent behavior.[34] Labels that are consistently applied, especially to a growing and evolving child or adolescent, contribute significantly to one's definition of "self."

To avoid the pitfalls of negative labels, shift the focus from the *actor* to the *act*. For example, suppose a child is throwing a tantrum. We could tell the child, "You're a bad boy," or we could say, "Your behavior is bad." The second statement addresses what the child is *doing*, while the first statement is more global, addressing *who he is*—always and everywhere. This communication can be improved by identifying the specific undesirable behavior: "Kicking and screaming is bad behavior." This pinpoints the unacceptable behavior and transfers the negative label from the child to the behavior. Focus on the act, not the actor.

Seminal research by Rosenthal and Jacobson showed that giving children an ability label can have a powerful effect on their caregivers' behavior, changing the way children are treated by others.[35] Teachers in an elementary school were told some of their students were top scorers on a test designed to identify students who would experience a period of intense intellectual development over the next year (i.e., "academic bloomers"). In reality, the students were randomly selected and were no different from the rest of the class.

A year later, the "bloomers" outperformed their peers by 10 to 15 IQ points. It was suggested that the teachers had unknowingly treated these "bloomers" differently, fostering greater academic development. This phenomenon of treating a labeled person in a way consistent with the label is known as the self-fulfilling prophecy—a powerful method of social influence.[36] The child is "sloppy"; the parent is "overly permissive"; the student is "ignorant"; the athlete is "lazy"; the perpetrator is inherently "evil"; or the worker is "careless."

This type of judgmental delivery does more harm than good. Substantial research demonstrates dramatic disadvantages of giving labels to people that go beyond their behavior or their effort, even when the label is positive.[19]

It's essential to separate behavior from person-states when giving and receiving feedback. Corrective feedback should not indict a child's personality or indicate a character flaw. Feedback must not relate to the child's attitude, motivation, competence, or family history. Feedback should focus strictly on observed behavior.

Sure, if a child responds well to supportive or corrective feedback it can lead to improved attitude, motivation, competence, and even a better person-state. But you provide feedback for only one reason: to pinpoint desired and/or undesired behavior. When this is realized by those who give and receive feedback, the benefits of behavioral coaching are maximized. There's room for improvement in most everything we do. But, only by receiving and accepting **behavior-based feedback** can we do better.

It's in the Delivery

Giving interpersonal feedback at the right time certainly increases its beneficial impact on behavior. Actually, timing is one of four basic guidelines we recommend you consider when planning your feedback strategies with children. These rules of feedback delivery are readily remembered with the key words: *specific, on time, appropriate,* and *real*. Note the first letters spell "soar." Follow these four basics of feedback delivery and you will "soar" to success with the young people you COACH.

Specific

As we've discussed, your feedback must focus on specific behavior. As a *consequence* (for motivation), your feedback specifies the behavior(s) to keep performing or the behavior(s) to stop performing. And as an *activator* (or directive), parenting or teaching with feedback reminds a child or youngster to perform a particular task in a certain way. This guidance needs to be given using straightforward and objective words and is referred to as **feedforward**.

Figure 3.4 illustrates the **activator-behavior-consequence (ABC)** model of ABS. Note the distinction between feedforward and feedback depicted in this diagram. Both of these behavior-improvement techniques need to be understood and accepted. People—especially children in different developmental stages—can obviously misperceive, misunderstand, or deny feedforward or feedback.

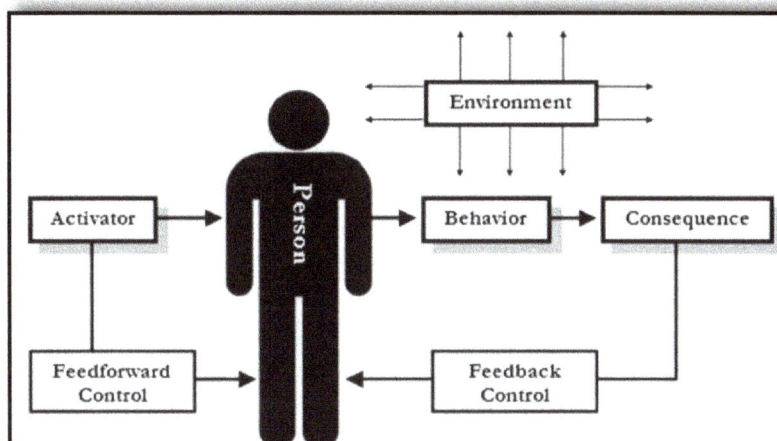

FIGURE 3.4   The ABC model of ABS that distinguishes feedforward from feedback.

The principles discussed here suggest ways to ensure that behavioral direction (feedforward) and behavioral support or correction (feedback) are approved and appreciated—yes, even by teenagers.

Ambiguous and subjective language about internal person-states is not useful when communicating to children and adolescents whose abilities to communicate and understand are evolving and not fully formed. In fact, it can be counterproductive. Think about the impact of evaluations that point out, "You're careless, lazy, unenthusiastic, unaware, disorganized, or out-of-touch." These types of statements are resented and lessen the acceptability of the behavioral message. And this is important: When you deliver *positive* statements, watch for the use of that infamous caveat—*but*.

Parents often feel obligated to add a negative statement to balance praise or appreciation. "I like the way you cleaned your room on your own without being told, *but* next time try to be more thoughtful about where you put your belongings." This kind of mixed message weakens your feedback. Some kids hear only the negative and miss the positive. Others discount both messages, figuring one positive and one negative equals no communication.

Make your specific behavior-focused feedback short and sweet. Don't combine supportive and corrective feedback in one exchange or overload a person with several behaviors to continue or change. Instead, concentrate your advice on one area of performance. Give children several concise and specific feedback messages, rather than fewer but longer feedback sessions with mixed and potentially confusing motives and directives.

Longer feedback sessions equal lectures, and we all know how children and teenagers react to lectures: as if they are forced to sit through a sermon of sorts or watch only black and white TV. One of the reasons social media is so overwhelmingly popular with the youth is the immediate feedback they receive after posting a photograph, video, or comment. Yes, it *is* all about soon, certain, and positive consequences.

On Time

As we've discussed, motivational feedback to increase or decrease how often behavior occurs should follow the target behavior as soon as possible. This is especially true for children, who live in the present and for whom attention span is limited.[4] A behavior is most likely to occur when it's followed by a *soon,*

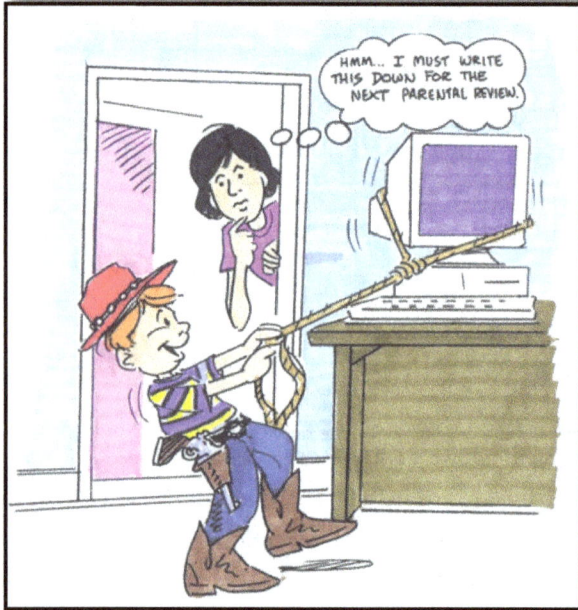

FIGURE 3.5   Identify misbehaviors as soon as possible.

certain, and *significant* consequence. Again, consider the immediacy of social media. Comments and reviews aren't posted days later, but rather seconds and minutes later.

As illustrated in Figure 3.5, waiting until a later time to address a behavioral problem is not recommended. Reward charts, as discussed earlier under Life Lesson 1, are an effective way to increase the occurrence of children's desired behavior. They provide visible evidence of success deserving of supportive feedback. Obviously, parents and caretakers need to use their verbal behavior to connect the information on a reward chart with supportive feedback.

Consistency

Supportive and corrective feedback should be consistent. This is especially true when a young person is learning a new task. This is a crucial guideline for parents and other caregivers. Many consider consistency a cardinal rule of effective parenting,[37] whether the behavioral feedback is supportive or corrective.[38] Giving feedback or other consequences (positive or negative) inconsistently is unfortunately one of the most common mistakes made by parents and other caregivers. Such inconsistency often occurs with the same caregiver (e.g., "Yesterday Mom scolded me for making a mess, but today she didn't say anything") or between different caregivers (e.g., "Dad gives me $5 for a good report card, but Mom says the satisfaction of the good grades is my reward").

On the other hand, if the purpose of behavioral feedback is to shape the quality of a response, it usually makes most sense to deliver this directive feedback as an activator (i.e., feedforward) preceding the next opportunity to perform the target behavior.

Timing Feedforward

Discussing an error as a consequence can be perceived as punishing and frustrating if an opportunity to correct the observed error does not present itself in the near future. When the opportunity to correct the behavior eventually arrives, the advice might be forgotten. Timing matters. When you time your advice in close proximity to the next opportunity for the desired behavior to recur (i.e., as feedforward), you increase its directive influence and reduce the potential of a negative attitude—such as denial or resentment—that results from catching a person making a mistake.

Suppose, for example, you observe a student walking hurriedly down a flight of stairs without using the handrail. Realizing the relatively high frequency of injuries caused by slips, trips, and falls, you see an opportunity to actively care for this person's safety. Should you provide corrective feedback?

Well, it's obvious this individual is in a hurry and would not appreciate a conversation about handrail use at this time. Plus, you might feel awkward providing corrective feedback in this context, with no credible opportunity to buffer the negative with relevant positive words. The solution: Offer behavioral feedforward.

In this case, *on time* means you wait for an opportunity to provide this individual with a feedforward reminder to use the handrail before s/he uses a flight of stairs. Yes, it may take some time before you can seize the feedforward moment. You might see an opportunity for this pre-behavior reminder when you and the target for your intervention are walking with a group of students. Now you simply say, "Let's remember to use the handrail." Of course, some situations involve more imminent danger (e.g., a student walking across the street while looking down at his/her cell phone and a car is approaching), in which case immediate feedback is necessary. But when given the choice, feedforward is often most effective.

Implicate Consequences

A feedforward directive is more likely to increase the frequency of the desired target behavior if it includes, or at least implies, a positive consequence the behavior provides or a negative consequence the behavior avoids. In the handrail example, the avoidance of falling is implicated, but it could be useful to add a consequence-relevant statement like, "Trips, slips, and falls are a most frequent cause of injuries, and using a handrail will prevent such a mishap."

Incidentally, we have seen a significant increase in the use of stairs without using a handrail at our universities. Smartphone talking and texting almost 24/7 is a lifestyle, occurring even when using stairs, crossing streets, and, most unfortunately, while driving. We periodically see a line of students walking down a flight of stairs rather slowly because a lead student is texting and walking slowly to concentrate and to compensate for the perceived risk. And, relatively few students in line behind this laggard are using the handrail.

Feedback to the texting student is certainly called for in this situation, and the consequence of holding up a line of other students could be stated as an observed negative consequence. If it's awkward to give feedback to this student at the time, one could certainly describe the situation to a group or class as feedforward—and with this student in the group or class. We have done this in our classes more than once.

The power of adding a potential consequence to feedforward directions is demonstrated in Figure 3.6. And, yes, Scott actually placed that sign on the vehicle his daughter was driving to her high school after she passed her driving exam at age 16. Do you think the potential consequence of a phone call increased the safe driving of his daughter?

Well, we will never know because, as the illustration shows, Krista did not like this idea and never drove that car with the sign in place. She did not buy in to her father's justification that a positive phone call is just as likely as a negative phone call. "Let's be optimistic about this," Scott said to her, "and see she how many positive phone calls I get about your safe and courteous driving behavior."

"Are you kidding me, Dad? There's no way I'd park that car and sign at my high school," Krista

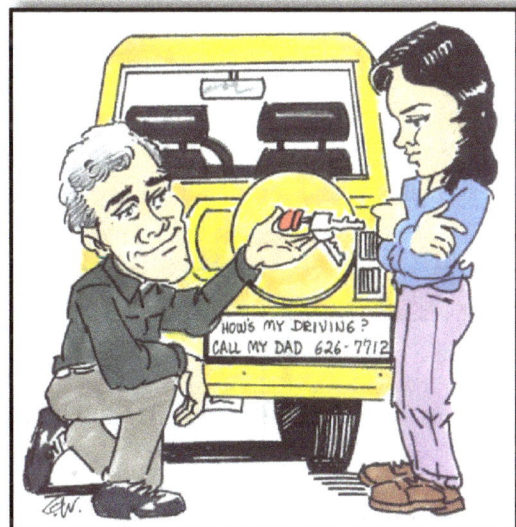

FIGURE 3.6   Activate behavior with a consequence.

retorted. "I'd be the laughingstock of the whole school. I'll talk to Mom about this." So, then there were unplanned behavioral consequences following that feedforward sign.

Appropriate

Specific and well-timed feedforward and feedback need to be tailored to the needs, abilities, and expectations of the person receiving direction, support, or correction. Simply put, feedforward and feedback should fit the situation, as well as the developmental stage of the child or adolescent. Feedforward and feedback should be expressed in language the child can understand and appreciate, and communication should be customized for the individual's ability to perform the particular task. Not until age three do children have the cognitive ability to learn from behavioral feedforward and feedback, but parents and caregivers can certainly give each other feedforward and feedback to make their interactions with children as appropriate and effective as possible.

Developmental Stage

As mentioned, providing behavioral feedforward and feedback for children requires consideration of the child's developmental stage. Children experience many physical, cognitive, and emotional changes throughout early childhood. These changes present particular challenges for parents and caregivers, and they determine the kind of behavior-change communication most appropriate. Figure 3.7 lists certain developmentally appropriate behavioral challenges and responsibilities typical of early childhood. In addition to growing two to three inches per year, children in early childhood develop gross motor skills (e.g., running, catching, throwing) as well as fine motor skills (e.g., using eating utensils, dressing themselves).[39]

Cognitively, children in early childhood are in what Jean Piaget called the *preoperational* stage of development, which is characterized by two substages.[4] Between 2 and 4 years of age, children develop *symbolic function*: the ability to remember, understand, and replicate objects in their mind. This ability to understand that one thing can represent something else means children at this age can begin to understand an if-then reward contingency (Life Lesson 1) and benefit from incentive/reward programs. However, there is wide variability within this 2- to 4-year period, making it important to assess a child's symbolic function. Expecting children to understand and comply with a request (i.e., feedforward) that is beyond their cognitive ability will lead to disappointment and can spur shame and self-doubt.

The preoperational stage is also a time of *egocentrism*. Children see the world from their perspective and are generally unable to take the perspective of others. This likely contributes to some of the interpersonal challenges typical of early childhood (e.g., difficulty in sharing).

The second substage of the preoperational stage occurs between 4 and 7 years of age. Children develop *intuitive thought* at this time. Cognitive processes progress from holding

Challenges	Responsbilities
• Testing Limits	• Homework
• Sleep/Wake Times	• Household Chores
• Eating	• Sharing
• Toilet Training	• Self-Care
• Tantrums	

FIGURE 3.7 Typical challenges and responsibilities for children in early childhood.

magical beliefs to rational beliefs, and children can appreciate dual relationships, understanding that something can be an object itself *and* a symbol for something else. These developments improve children's understanding of if-then contingencies, allowing them to take a more collaborative role in developing and implementing basic incentive/reward programs (e.g., use of the reward chart, Lesson 1), as well as understanding progressively more complex behavioral-improvement plans.

Language requires both physical and cognitive abilities, and these also change dramatically throughout early childhood. Language development influences behavior and should be considered in understanding early childhood behavior and applying feedforward and feedback. For example, a toddler's inability to adequately express her wants and needs can result in frustration, serving as an antecedent to undesirable behavior. Similarly, interventions relying too much on verbal behavior can fall flat with a 5-year-old who has good verbal expression but still has limited comprehension.

Children with Special Needs
Some children have emotional or cognitive challenges, in addition to the developmental factors influencing all children. These challenges need to be considered when planning and delivering feedforward, feedback, and other behavior-improvement tactics. The direct, present-focused nature of ABS intervention makes it ideal for children with learning disorders, as well as for those who have compromised cognitive abilities.

Attention deficit/hyperactivity disorder (ADHD) and autism spectrum disorder (ASD) are discussed here as examples of conditions that impact early childhood behavior and have been most successfully addressed with ABS. It's estimated that 5% of the children in the United States meet the diagnostic criteria for attention deficit/hyperactivity disorder.[40] An accurate diagnosis cannot be made before age 7, but children often show signs in early childhood.

Both inattention and hyperactivity impact which behaviors should be targeted, as well as the intervention strategies used. For example, a child who struggles with hyperactivity may not be able to follow the command, "Sit still and stay in your chair until dinner is over." It would be more realistic for this child to remain seated while eating but have a break during the dinner period in order to get out of his/her seat and "get some wiggles out." Again, in the spirit of **humanistic behaviorism** we need to customize a behavior-improvement process for each particular child.

The field of applied behavior analysis or applied behavioral science (ABS) has addressed the special needs of children with developmental disabilities in general and autism spectrum disorder in particular for more than 60 years.[41] ASD is a neurodevelopmental disorder present in early childhood, characterized by significant problems with social, emotional, and communication skills.[40] This disorder is diagnosed in early childhood, with diagnosis made as early as 2 years of age and remaining fairly stable throughout childhood.[42] Research consistently shows ABS intervention to be the most effective method for managing the behaviors of children with ASD.[43] Consequently, ABS intervention that provides appropriate behavioral direction (feedforward) and support (feedback) has become the treatment of choice for ASD.[44]

Other Considerations
Let's consider for a moment the developmental stages of older children—preteen, teenagers, and young adults in college or working but still living at home. Emotions roll up and down like a roller coaster. Hormones are running wild. Peer pressure, social media, and the stress to succeed

academically and perhaps athletically often weigh heavily on these more-developed, but still evolving, older children.

Parental intervention at these stages can be particularly challenging. Rebellious, egocentric, or independent-minded behavior can be typical. At this stage of parenting, authentic caring, coaching, empathic support, and direct or indirect advice are critical. The need for corrective feedback will often come into play with teenagers. Indeed, effective feedforward and supportive and corrective feedback are critical when your child is making life decisions such as choosing a college or a career.

When children or adults are taught a task—whether learning to use a computer or mobile device, ride a bicycle, or drive a car—directive behavior-focused feedforward and supportive feedback need to be detailed and perhaps accompanied with a behavioral demonstration. In these learning situations, it's important to align your advice with the individual's achievement level. Don't expect too much at once, and don't overload more advice than the performer can grasp in one feedforward exchange.

At times, people exhibit subpar behavior even when they know how to perform the task well. They might have developed suboptimal habits or are just taking a shortcut for efficiency. Detailed instructions about the best way to complete a task can feel insulting and demeaning to a person who is experienced at the particular task. In these situations, it's best to give feedforward as a reminder to take extra time for effectiveness over efficiency. You want quality, not expediency. Preceding your reminder with the words, "As you know," increases acceptance of the reminder.

Bear in mind, as a humanistic-behavioral parent and/or coach you need to size up the situation. Make your specific and timely feedforward or feedback fit the occasion. This is not easy and requires an up-to-date awareness of the performer's knowledge and skill regarding a certain task. You also need specific knowledge of the optimal ways to perform a task in a given situation. This is why the most effective behavioral coaching usually occurs between individuals serving on the same team (or in the same family), or at least between people acquainted with each other's skills and the task calling for feedforward and/or feedback.

Real

Interpersonal coaching is most effective when it is perceived as genuine and caring. Authenticity is quite popular and prized today among teenagers and young adults. Feedforward and feedback are ineffective if the verbal behavior is viewed as exerting top-down control, or implying superior knowledge, competence, or motivation. Improving and sustaining the competence of children, teens, colleagues, or team members is the sole reason for giving behavioral feedforward or feedback.

Although well-intended, the **discipline** policies in some organizations (consider a family or a classroom to be a form of "organization") make it difficult for some people to view corrective feedback as caring and supporting. It might be well intentioned, but the "gotcha" mindset associated with "rule enforcement" can interfere with a person's sincere attempt to correct another individual's suboptimal performance. Of course, we're now talking about managing the behavior of adolescents and/or providing feedforward and feedback for parents and other caregivers.

Corrective feedback regarding the improvement of caregiving behavior is most likely to be received as genuine or *real* when it occurs between peers—other parents or caregivers. Peers possess the most intimate knowledge of a situation and the person(s) involved, and thus they have sufficient information and opportunity to make feedforward and feedback specific, on time, appropriate, and real.

While younger children are quite attentive to direct feedforward and feedback from their parents, and are usually eager to please them by demonstrating appropriate behavior, this is often not the case for the preteens, teens, and young adults. Now the peer group takes preferential control, and this can be extremely challenging and frustrating. You can hope that the fundamentals you provided your child early on will influence the selection of a peer group, or perhaps some of your early parenting and mentoring will take precedence over undesirable choices. Still, you can have significant influence over the behavior, attitudes, values, and success of your children throughout their lives by following the humanistic behaviorism principles presented and illustrated in the life lessons.

Summary

We've reviewed key guidelines for delivering effective interpersonal feedforward and feedback. The acronym "SOAR" is a useful teaching/learning tool, because each letter of this acronym reflects a key word that implicates a guideline for delivering feedforward and feedback effectively: *specific*, *on time*, *appropriate*, and *real*.

SOAR indicates the special value of parents and caregivers giving children effective feedforward and feedback. Parents and caregivers have complete knowledge of the feedforward/feedback recipient and the situation. They are positioned to make their behavioral feedforward and feedback: (a) *specific* in terms of behavior to initiate, continue, or stop; (b) *appropriate* for the knowledge, abilities, and experiences of the child; (c) *on time* for observable connections between a behavior and an activator and consequence; and (d) reflect *real* concern for the child's competence and performance goals.

When intervening on behalf of children's well-being it's particularly critical to be *on time* with feedforward or feedback. Whether you use feedback to support desirable behavior or decrease the occurrence of undesirable behavior, *on time* means your feedback should be delivered as a consequence that follows the observed behavior as soon as possible.

In contrast, when using feedforward to encourage certain behavior (perhaps as a correction for subpar behavior observed earlier) you should consider your communication to be a reminder or an activator. Wait for a situation that calls for the particular behavior and then offer a specific, appropriate, and genuine reminder. Appropriate interpersonal feedforward or feedback enables you to "soar" to new heights of parenting, teaching, coaching, and interpersonal effectiveness.

Discussion Questions

It's extremely useful to discuss these four guidelines for giving feedforward and feedback in situations relevant for caregivers and children. The format to connect these principles with realistic applications can vary markedly. An instructor could solicit comments from all participants. Or, participants could be divided into small groups; then after the questions and issues posed here are discussed, a representative from each group could report their perspectives to the entire assembly of participants.

Whatever protocol you employ to encourage an interactive discussion of feedforward and feedback, consider the following questions. It would be optimal for learning if you would write personal reactions to these questions before discussing them with one or more other parents or caregivers.

1. How have you used interpersonal feedforward and feedback to improve the behavior of a young child? Please explain.

_____

_____

_____

_____

2. What factors hold you back from giving a young person behavior-focused feedforward or feedback? Please explain with reference to a particular person and situation.

_____

_____

_____

_____

3. How might you overcome a barrier to giving a young person behavior-improvement feedforward or feedback?

_____

_____

_____

_____

4. Describe a personal experience in which you *received* behavior-focused feedforward or feedback from a caregiver, teacher, supervisor, coach, or colleague. How was this exchange appropriate or inappropriate with regard to the SOAR guidelines?

_____

_____

_____

_____

5. Describe a personal experience in which you delivered behavior-focused feedforward or feedback to a young child. How was this communication appropriate or inappropriate with regard to the SOAR guidelines?

_____

_____

_____

_____

6. Describe the last time you gave a young child feedback to support or recognize a desirable (e.g., AC4P) behavior you observed.

_____

_____

_____

_____

Use More Supportive than Corrective Feedback*

"We can't learn unless we make mistakes." How many times have you heard this? Yes, this perspective or paradigm might make us feel better about the errors of our ways. Perhaps you've given your kids this consoling advice after they made an embarrassing error. But nothing could be further from the truth. Behavioral scientists have shown convincingly that success—not failure—produces the most efficient and effective learning.[45]

At the start of the last century, Edward Lee Thorndike put chickens, cats, dogs, fish, monkeys, and humans in situations that called for problem solving. He was studying intelligence. Thorndike systematically observed how these organisms learned. The "Law of Effect" was his term to describe the fact that learning depends on behavioral consequences.[46] His key finding: Markedly more learning occurred following positive consequences (success) than negative consequences (failure).

Given this finding, does an error need to occur in order to solve a problem? You can reflect on your own experiences—or that of your children—to answer this question. A pleasant consequence directs and motivates you to continue the behavior. You know what you did to receive the reward, and you're motivated to earn another.

A negative consequence following a mistake only tells you what not to do. It provides no specific direction for problem solving. You can be frustrated and discouraged when a mistake you made is overemphasized; it could actually de-motivate you to continue the learning process. Sometimes a soon, certain,

---

* Portions of this chapter originally appeared in A. K. Fournier, K. England Will, & K. Larson, "Actively caring for our children," in E. S. Geller (Ed.), Applied psychology: Actively caring for people (pp. 469–505). Copyright © 2016 by E. Scott Geller. Reprinted by permission of Cambridge University Press.

and significant negative consequence is useful to emphasize the impropriety of intolerable behavior (e.g., driving while intoxicated, texting while driving, or staying out beyond a specified curfew); but even under these circumstances, constructive mentoring, corrective action discussion and planning, is necessary to direct and motivate the performance of the appropriate alternative.

Errors are not necessary for learning to occur. In fact, when **education** or training results in no errors, learning is a most smooth and enjoyable process.[45] Errors disrupt the teaching/learning process and can lead to a negative attitude, especially if negative social consequences accentuate the mistake. Even subtle reactions to an error—a disappointed face or verbal tone—can increase feelings of helplessness or despair and turn off a person to the entire learning process.

Delivering Supportive Feedback

Supportive feedback is the most powerful positive consequence to construct and sustain a successful learning process. It's the theme of this discussion. Still, some attempts to be positive and supportive are ineffective, as Figure 4.1 shows. Therefore, we now provide basic guidelines for delivering quality supportive feedback.

Be Timely

As we emphasized in Life Lesson 3, to provide optimal direction and encouragement, supportive feedback needs to connect directly with the desired behavior, as *not* demonstrated in Figure 4.1. When children know what they did to earn appreciation, they are likely to be motivated to continue that behavior.

If it's necessary to delay the supportive feedback, your conversation should relive the activity deserving recognition. Talk specifically about the behavior that warrants special acknowledgement. Don't hesitate to ask the feedback recipient to recall aspects of the situation and the commendable behavior. This enables you to direct and motivate the person to continue his/her desired behavior. Of course, the level of recognition communication depends on the age and developmental stage of the recipient of recognition, as discussed in Life Lesson 3.

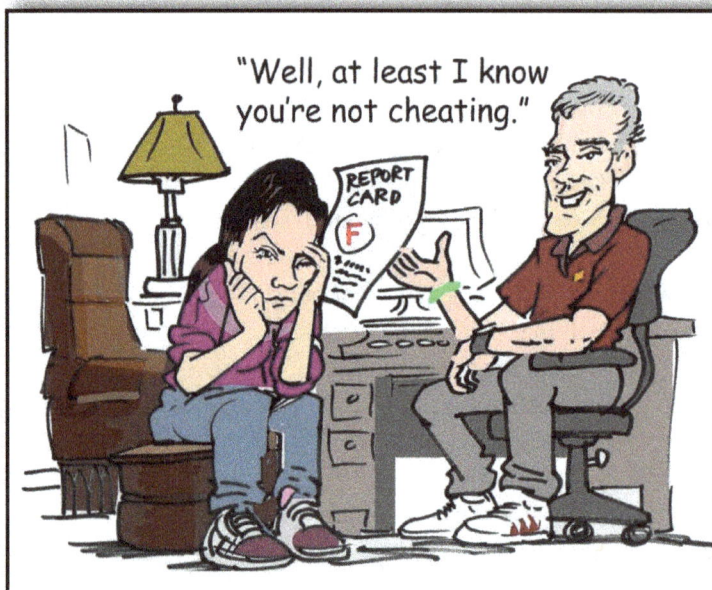

FIGURE 4.1 Dad's attempt to be positive misses the mark.

Make it Personal

Supportive feedback is most meaningful when it's perceived as personal. Your verbal support should not be vague or generic, applicable for any situation, as in "Nice job!" Customize it to fit a particular individual and circumstance. This happens naturally when the supportive feedback is linked to a designated behavior. When you recognize someone, you're expressing personal thanks. "Thanks for taking our dog for a walk."

At times it's tempting to say, "*We* appreciate" rather than "*I* appreciate," and to refer to gratitude of a group or team rather than *personal appreciation*. But speaking for a team can come across as impersonal and insincere.

It's appropriate, naturally, to reflect an individual's value to a team or family when you give supportive feedback, but your focus should be personal: "I saw what you did to support the class and I really appreciate it. *Your example demonstrates the kind of leadership we need around here.*" This second statement illustrates the next guideline for giving quality supportive feedback. Of course, we're referring to feedback conversations with older children, or with other parents or caregivers.

Take it to a Higher Level

When your supportive feedback reflects a higher-order quality, it's most memorable and inspirational. Add a universal positive such as **leadership**, integrity, trustworthiness, or AC4P to your recognition statement and you make your feedback more meaningful and rewarding. It's important to state the specific behavior first, and then make an obvious linkage between the behavior and the positive characteristic it reflects.

This is how you bring interpersonal supportive feedback to a higher level of effectiveness: positively impacting the recipient's self-esteem, competence, and sense of **interdependence** and **belongingness**. Later, under Life Lesson 6, we explain how these person-states enhance self-motivation and the propensity to perform more AC4P behavior.

Social Labels

Under Life Lesson 1, we discussed the importance of labeling *effort* or behavior over *ability* (e.g., inherently intelligent or athletic). This is because people want to live up to the labels given to them by others, especially their peer group and the parents they look up to, as well as respected teachers and coaches. Most young children try hard to gain the approval of their parents and caregivers, and this often means fulfilling the positive expectations provided by a social label.

Social psychologists have shown that people attempt to behave consistently with *reasonable* labels given to them.[47] By now you realize that a reasonable label is one connected specifically to achievable behaviors implied by the label. Thus, when you take supportive feedback to a higher level, you are recognizing the kind of behavior that warrants the positive label given the individual.

If the feedback recipient considers the social label worthwhile or important, s/he will attempt to perform behavior that reflects the label. With young children, teaching desirable behaviors relevant to a positive social label is a critical responsibility of parents and caregivers. Children need to learn the value of various positive social labels (e.g., honest, fair, friendly, diligent, grateful, and helpful), as well as the achievable behaviors that represent a particular social label. Such labeling comes from verbal conversations and/or demonstrations of the parent/caregiver and can come across as parent controlled or other directed.[48] What if the positive social label is perceived as self-directed?[48] We call this self-labeling.

Self-Labels

In the Life Lesson 6, we cover the topic of self-direction or self-motivation, and we explain how to achieve this enviable person-state in ourselves and in our children. We initiate this discussion here by considering the value of acquiring a self-label, and then we explain how to facilitate the personal adoption of a positive self-label.

First, it's intuitive that the ownership of a positive label and the commitment to perform behaviors reflecting that label is strongest when the behavior-based label is perceived as self-directed—a *self-label*. So, how can a parent or caregiver facilitate the development of a positive self-label?

The answer is also intuitive. Every reader has developed a self-label, and the process connects directly to the issue of self-motivation, discussed later in Life Lesson 6. It's all about involvement and perceived competence. When individuals of any age get involved in a task they perceive as worthwhile and feel competent at completing that task successfully, they give themselves a positive self-label that reflects their achievement. How do you increase a person's perception of competence and facilitate positive self-labeling? The answer is, of course, supportive behavioral feedback.

Here's an example of a child's involvement that led to a self-label and subsequent desirable behavior consistent with that label. In 1984, when Scott's daughter Karly was three and a half, she implemented an intervention to increase the safety-belt use of vehicle drivers, termed "the flash for life." The intervention is depicted in Figure 4.2, which illustrates the ABC model discussed earlier under Life Lesson 3 (see Figure 3.4).

Karly's driver (mom or dad) pulled up to intersections in the left lane so the driver in the adjacent vehicle was clearly visible. If the driver did not have the shoulder strap buckled, which was typical in 1984, Karly held up the front side of a bright yellow-and-white flash card with the feedforward message in bold lettering: "Please Buckle Up—I Care." If the driver buckled up on the spot, which happened on 37 of 154 flashes, Karly flipped over the sign with the positive feedback message: "Thank You for Buckling Up."[49]

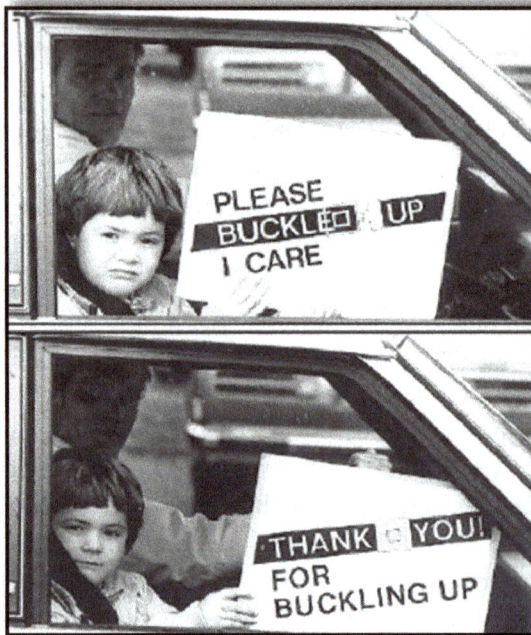

FIGURE 4.2 Karly prompting an unbuckled driver (top) and thanking a driver for buckling up.

While this story illustrates the positive impact of a simple feedforward intervention, we share it here as an illustration of the impact of self-labeling. Not only did young Karly always buckle up in a vehicle, she was quick to remind all other occupants of vehicles in which she was a passenger to buckle their safety belt. And she always said "safety belt," not seatbelt. She had seemingly developed the self-label of "safety-belt-use promoter." Furthermore, Karly's early involvement in this *community* intervention to promote safety-belt use led to a self-label that generalized to other safety-related behaviors consistent with that self-label (e.g., wearing the proper protective helmet when biking, motorcycling, and horseback riding).

Thus, it's advantageous to provide young children with opportunities to participate in programs that reflect a positive social label (e.g., community efforts to serve disadvantaged people, conserve environmental resources, and promote AC4P behavior). A self-motivated self-label might very well result from such involvement and thereby activate subsequent occurrences of desirable behaviors consistent with that positive self-label.

These self-labels can be further reinforced when desired behavior is recognized by important others. When Karly was in fourth grade, she actually won first prize in a speech contest by relating her early experiences with the "flash for life" intervention. And when she was 12, Karly implemented the "airline lifesaver" by handing an airline attendant on a flight from Puerto Rico a note with the following announcement request, "Now that the safest part of your trip is over, the flight crew would like to remind you to buckle up during your ground transportation." As it turned out, when the plane landed Karly was invited to read this buckle-up reminder over the PA system, and she did. Her AC4P message was followed by an enthusiastic applause from the passengers—more support for Karly's self-label.

What about tasks children might view as boring or worthless, like cleaning up their room, doing the dishes, watching a younger sibling, or running an errand? Can such involvement in unpleasant tasks lead to a positive self-label? Well again, it's all about the delivery of positive labeling by the parent. If the task is described as a special opportunity and rewarded with words of sincere praise, a positive self-label could result. You're not just "washing the dishes," you're the "chef's special assistant and practicing a life-long skill." You're not just "watching your younger sister," you're "her official guardian, looking out for her well-being and making sure she doesn't get hurt."

Deliver it Privately

Supportive feedback needs to be delivered privately and one on one because it is personal and indicative of higher-order attributes. You should also consider this: Your verbal support is special and only relevant to one person. Thus, it's more meaningful and genuine if you deliver it personally—from one parent or caregiver to one child.

Recognizing individuals in front of a group is a tradition. It's typified in athletic contests and reflects the pop-psychology slogan, "Praise publicly and reprimand privately." Many teachers and coaches take their lead from this commonsense statement and recognize their students or athletes in group settings.

To be held up as an exemplar before one's peers is maximally rewarding, right? Not necessarily. Individuals of all ages can feel embarrassed when singled out in front of a group. This could be out of fear of later harassment by peers. The recognized individual might be degraded as a "teacher's pet" or "brownnoser," or accused of "sucking up to the teacher or the boss." Even receiving public praise among family members can be suboptimal if it occurs in the presence of siblings who sense a win/lose rivalry.

For example, when Scott was in third grade, his teacher recognized him in front of the class for doing "the best job" on his homework. He was very embarrassed, as depicted in Figure 4.3. After school, a gang of boys gave him a playground beating. Unfortunately, that teacher never received feedback about this negative consequence of her public recognition.

FIGURE 4.3 Public recognition can do more harm than good.

Athletic performance is measured objectively, and winners are determined fairly and duly recognized. But in most school and work settings, it can be impossible to assess everyone's relevant behaviors objectively and obtain a fair ranking for individual recognition. Praising one individual in public may be perceived as favoritism by those who feel they did equally well but did not get praised. In the context of sibling rivalry, most have heard something like, "Oh you're Mom's favorite" or "Dad always liked you more."

Public appraisal also sets up a win-lose atmosphere. This may be appropriate for some sporting contests, but not when the desirable family mission is to promote a cooperative interdependent culture of optimal teaching and learning. It's beneficial, of course, to recognize a team of children for their accomplishment, and this *can* be done in a group setting. Since individual responsibility is diffused or dispersed across the group, there is minimal risk of embarrassing someone or activating peer harassment.

We're not only talking about sports and academics here. Sometime the entire family unit does something praiseworthy. "That was a great vacation. We all got along really well, even on the rainy days. We'll definitely do that again. Thanks."

It's important to realize, though, that group achievement is rarely democratic, resulting from the equal input of all team members. Some take the lead and work harder; others "coast" and count on the group effort to make them shine. And even with equal levels of competence and motivation, experience and effort vary greatly. Thus, it's important to personally and privately recognize the young people who go beyond what's asked of them for the sake of their team. It's the same for families. When one sibling contributes most to a family project, s/he should receive one-on-one interpersonal recognition.

Let it Sink in

We live in an accelerated age of doing more with less. All parents know how over-scheduled their kids are these days—all the homework they're given, the pressures they face to succeed in the classroom ("Gotta get those AP courses"), on the playing field ("Gotta get that scholarship"), or in other pursuits ("Maybe if you're good enough during rehearsal, you can get to perform that solo"). So, we tend to overcompensate when communicating with others.

After we recognize a child for performing a desired behavior, we're tempted to tag on a bunch of unrelated statements, sometimes a request for additional behavior. This comes across as, "I appreciate your effort, but I need more." Resist this temptation. Simply praise the desirable behavior you observed. If you have additional points to discuss, it's best to reconnect later, after your supportive feedback has had a chance to sink in and become part of the individual's self-talk for self-recognition and self-motivation.

When you give supportive recognition, you give kids a script to use for rewarding their own behavior. Supportive feedback strengthens the child's self-reward system. This positive self-talk (or self-recognition) is critical for long-term maintenance of desired behavior. By allowing your supportive feedback to stand alone and be personally absorbed, you enable internalization of rewarding self-talk that can be used later as self-motivation to perform the recognized behavior again.

Use Tangibles for Symbolic Value

Tangible rewards can detract from the self-motivating feature of quality recognition. If a material reward is the focus of an AC4P recognition process, words of appreciation are diminished in value. Self-motivation is stifled.

In Figure 4.4, Billy is expecting an extrinsic reward for his successful academic performance. In this case, his expected prize is directing him away from the most meaningful positive consequence: He solved the math problem. The teacher *should* focus Billy's attention on the fruits of his labor: his correct solution of the problem. Such positive recognition for a job well done is more memorable and more likely than an extra reward to facilitate self-motivation, as we discuss in Life Lesson 6.

Parents sometime use incentives/rewards to motivate their kids to do the right thing. Money is often used as an incentive to get good grades or perform well in sports. The kids know they're being incentivized, and the reward has limited long-term effect. But tangible rewards delivered as tokens of appreciation can add to the quality of interpersonal recognition.

Remember that how you deliver your tangible reward determines whether it adds or subtracts from the long-term sustainability of your praise. The benefit of interpersonal recognition is weakened if the tangible reward is perceived as a payoff—a bribe—for desired behavior. For example, a monetary incentive for reading a book might detract from the intrinsic value of reading. But if the reward is received as a token of appreciation for the desired behavior and not as a "pay off," it strengthens your praise.

FIGURE 4.4 Don't focus on extrinsic consequences.

Consider Secondhand Recognition

Up to now, we've discussed verbal communication in which you recognize a child or adolescent one on one for a particular behavior. You could also do this indirectly, and this approach comes with special advantages. Suppose, for example, you overhear a friend tell another person of your outstanding success as a parent. How does this secondhand recognition affect you? Do you believe the words of praise you overheard were genuine?

FIGURE 4.5 A recipient of praise may perceive an ulterior motive.

People can question the sincerity of praise when it's delivered face to face. Is there some ulterior motive? Perhaps a favor is expected in return, as shown in Figure 4.5. Or perhaps the recognition is devalued because it's perceived merely as a forced communication exercise: "She's just saying that to be nice." Secondhand recognition is not as easily tainted with these potential biases.

A mom telling her daughter she played beautifully at the piano recital will have a positive impact on the child, but secondhand recognition—reporting to her the positive reaction of an unknown audience member sitting next to her—might be considered more authentic. Because the success was reported to the parent rather than to the child, no ulterior motive exists for the indirect praise.

Plus, secondhand recognition can build a sense of belongingness or group cohesion among individuals. When you learn someone was bragging about your behavior, your sense of friendship with that person will likely increase.

Talking about children's achievement in behavior-specific terms can begin a cycle of positive communication that sustains desired behavior. This can help children develop the practice of positive self-talk, which begets self-recognition and self-motivation. Self-talk, also known as inner-speech or covert behavior, follows a developmental trajectory.

By age 2 or 3, children are developing language, and they begin to demonstrate *private* speech (talking aloud to themselves while engaging in an activity). This progresses from irrelevant speech to task-relevant speech (providing guidance and commentary) to *external* signs of *inner* speech (task-relevant whispering, inaudible murmuring). By adolescence, self-dialogue is mostly internal, with no external signs, and resembles self-talk as we're discussing it here.[51]

Take it upon yourself to initiate this cycle of positivity. Set an example for the kind of interpersonal communication that enhances self-esteem, **self-efficacy**, personal control, **optimism**, and group cohesion. These are the very person-states we want to cultivate in the next generation, and they do develop over the life span. Beginning in infancy, children develop a sense of self, self-esteem, and personal efficacy in response to the environment (including treatment and reactions from parents).[52] The advancement of these person-states is particularly vulnerable in childhood and adolescence, when parents control much of these young persons' environment.

Accept Supportive Feedback

Most of us are caught completely off guard when we're acknowledged for our commendable actions. Why? Because we get so little supportive feedback from others, we don't know how to digest this recognition when it finally comes. Or we've been taught that it's inappropriate or "bragging" to accept credit from others for our success. We should teach young people to not shy away when supportive feedback comes their way; instead, we hope they have the courage to embrace it.

As the first life lesson explained, positive consequences increase the odds that the recognized behavior will continue. Plus, how we react to supportive feedback influences whether the observer will try to give supportive feedback again. It's crucial to react appropriately when we receive recognition from others. Actually, young children usually accept recognition or supportive feedback well, with a genuine smile and no denial. Parents, guardians, and adolescents should model that behavior.

Let's consider seven basic guidelines for receiving supportive behavioral feedback well. Consistent with Life Lesson 2 (observational learning), while telling children about accepting feedback well is important, modeling the desirable behavior is probably the most important way to teach children how to accept supportive feedback.

Don't Deny or Disclaim

When we attempt to give supportive recognition, we often get a reaction that implies we're wasting our time. We hear disclaimers such as "It was really nothing special" or "Just doing my job." The most common reply these days is "No problem." This implies there was nothing special about the behavior and it didn't warrant supportive feedback. "No problem, Dad, I like raking leaves." "Thanks, but did you hear that bad note I hit during the recital?" "Yeah, it's a good report card, Mom, but aren't I supposed to get straight A's?"

Supportive feedback must be accepted without any denial or disclaimer. Plus, it should not deflect credit to others. Teach children and show by your example there's nothing wrong with taking pride in your small-win accomplishments, even if others contributed to the successful outcome. After all, the vision of an **AC4P culture** calls for everyone to perform **discretionary behavior** on behalf of the well-being of others. In this context, numerous people deserve recognition daily.

Supportive feedback will be intermittent at best for everyone; that's simply reality. So, children need to be taught that when their turn finally comes, they should accept the supportive feedback not only for the current behavior recognized, but for any prior desirable behaviors they performed that went unnoticed. Genuinely appreciating supportive feedback increases the chances the person who gave *you* feedback will give more behavioral recognition to *others*. Plus, you might be inspired to do the same. You realized a personal benefit from the recognition you received, and you want others to experience such positive behavioral support.

Listen Actively

Teach children to listen actively to the person who recognizes them with supportive feedback. Certainly, they want to learn what they did right. Plus, older children and adolescents can evaluate how well the supportive feedback is delivered. If the feedback does not pinpoint a particular behavior, they might ask the person, "What exactly did I do to deserve this?" This helps improve the person's method of giving supportive feedback.

Indeed, parents and guardians should teach young children to ask, "What did I do to deserve your special recognition?" in the event that the person giving supportive feedback does not specify the behavior warranting recognition. And finally, teach children to show genuine appreciation for special attention; this is obvious. Help them understand how difficult it is for many people to leave their comfort zones and recognize others with supportive feedback. Children should relish the fact that they're receiving recognition, even if its quality could be improved. Actually, this is true for all of us, right?

Use it Later for Self-Motivation

Help children realize that supportive feedback is well deserved whenever they do receive it. They perform many desirable behaviors when no one else is around. And even when others are present, these persons are usually so preoccupied with their own routines they don't catch another person's extra effort. "Think about all the times you are staying on task in class and your teacher is too busy working with other students to notice. The fact that she complimented your on-task behavior today is a big deal."

Teach children to relive the moment later and talk about it to themselves. Self-recognition can inspire them to be self-motivated and do more than what's expected. Self-talk helps to muster the motivation to perform more of the recognized behavior. Young children can certainly learn to use self-talk for self-motivation, and therefore adults should teach them this self-motivation technique.

Show Sincere Appreciation

Teach children to reciprocate with true gratitude—a smile, a "thank you," and perhaps special words such as "You've made my day." The reaction to supportive feedback can determine whether that parent or caregiver will deliver similar recognition again. Children should offer words that reflect their pleasure in this memorable positive interaction.

It's natural to add, "You've made my day" to the "thank you" because it's the truth. When people go out of their way to offer us quality recognition, they *have* made our day. In fact, we can teach youth to relive such situations to brighten up a later day.

Reward the Recognizer

When we accept supportive feedback well, we reward the person for his/her appreciative behavior. This can lead to delivering more positive feedback, especially if giving supportive feedback does not come naturally for the caregiver. You can do even more sometimes to assure the occurrence of more supportive feedback. Recognize the person for recognizing you. You might say, for example, "I really appreciate you noticing my behavior and offering sincere appreciation." Such supportive and rewarding feedback contributes to cultivating a culture of interpersonal compassion in which AC4P becomes a social norm.

Ask for Recognition

We can also teach children to ask for supportive feedback when they feel they deserve it. "How did I do at the recital, Dad?" Sure, this recognition will come off as less genuine than if it had been spontaneous, but the outcome can still be quite beneficial. The child might still hear some words worth reliving later for self-motivation. Most importantly, the child is reminding the caregiver in a polite way that s/he missed a prime opportunity to give supportive feedback. This could be a valuable learning experience for the adult.

Suppose a child tells a parent or caregiver how pleased s/he is with the outcome of his/her extra effort. Using the right tone and affect, this verbal behavior doesn't come across as bragging but declares pride in a small-win accomplishment. The parent or caregiver will surely support the self-praise with his/her own testimony, and this bolsters the child's self-motivation. Plus, it teaches the caregiver how to support the commendable behavior of others.

Parents, guardians, and caregivers for young children: We suggest you teach children from age 4 and older these techniques for receiving supportive feedback or recognition. In fact, the COACH principles explained in Life Lesson 3 should be used to teach others of all ages how to give and receive supportive feedback.

FIGURE 4.6 Positive recognition is too rare.

Satisfy the Craving

William James, the first renowned American psychologist, wrote, "The deepest principle in human nature is the craving to be appreciated" (p. 313).[53] In 1936, Dale Carnegie advocated, "Always make the other person feel important" as the key to winning friends and influencing people (p. 19).[54] How can we satisfy this human need to feel appreciated and important? The answer is, of course, to give and receive supportive feedback effectively. As depicted humorously in Figure 4.6, positive recognition from others can be rare yet sorely desired.

From Principles to Practice

Before you apply the interpersonal feedback techniques discussed here, we suggest you role-play procedures for delivering and receiving supportive and **corrective feedback**. Such practice could occur among parents and caregivers at workshops or group sessions to teach and promote effective positive parenting. Or, family members could actually hold practice sessions and discussions among themselves. Consider

FIGURE 4.7 Vital skill development takes time and effort.

having family discussions about giving and receiving more supportive feedback, and then having enjoyable role-play interactions, accompanied by frank and open feedback about ways to improve each interaction. This is an excellent way to become AC4P parents, guardians, caregivers, and siblings. Although this may seem like a lot to ask, we actually do more than this to prepare for other endeavors (like improving our golf game) with far-less-serious consequences.

Role-play exercises should be followed by systematic behavioral feedback from an instructor (or other participants). The delivery of this feedback should adhere to the guidelines presented here, thereby providing observational learning for all participants. We also recommend that participants practice appropriate feedback techniques on their family members before taking their behavior-improvement techniques to the "street."

Work on mastering *supportive* feedback before you attempt *corrective* feedback. It's much easier to deliver supportive feedback or behavioral recognition than corrective feedback. Supportive feedback can do no harm, even if it is applied incorrectly. On the other hand, inappropriate delivery of corrective feedback can result in resistance or hurt feelings on the part of the recipient that can interfere with future interactions.

After discussing the benefits of providing supportive and corrective feedback, an instructor or facilitator should review the basics of how to deliver supportive feedback to children and how children should receive such feedback, as detailed. Participants should pair off and practice giving each other supportive feedback. One participant should agree to be the feedback "sender" (i.e., the adult caregiver) and the other the "recipient" (i.e., the child). A particular situation and behavior should be defined for the role-play exercise. This can be a real-world situation caregivers have actually experienced or an imagined scenario that calls for behavioral feedback.

After receiving supportive feedback, recipients should express their reaction. Did the feedback seem genuine? Did it address a specific behavior? Did the recipient feel rewarded by the exchange? Then the roles should be reversed, with the "sender" playing the role of "recipient," and vice versa.

TABLE 4.1   Documentation of Delivering Supportive Feedback

Behavior Recognized	Environmental Setting	Reactions of Recipient
1. Ate vegetables without complaining	*Dinner table at home, Tuesday evening*	*Big smile, "Thanks, Dad"*
2.		
3.		
4.		
5.		

The instructor/facilitator should circulate among the practicing role-players and note examples of particularly effective and ineffective performance. These observations can then be discussed when the participants reconvene as a group. Group members should discuss their feedback experiences from the perspective of both the feedback sender and the recipient.

Group leaders might select a feedback pair who displayed exemplary performance during the role-play sessions and ask them to demonstrate their interaction skills to the rest of the group. The group facilitator might offer supportive and corrective feedback to the presenters, and then ask other participants to contribute their own supportive and corrective feedback.

After you gain confidence through role-playing your ability to "catch good behavior" and give genuine supportive feedback, be ready to reap the benefits of real-world experience. Observe the ongoing behaviors of young people in your home. After noting a "good" behavior, apply the supportive feedback process. Document your experience by completing Table 4.1; the first line is an example of the information to record. After completing this chart, discuss the information (especially children's reactions) at group meetings.

Giving Corrective Feedback

Role-playing, group demonstrations, and interactive feedback should be used to improve parent and caregiver skills at giving *corrective feedback*. Practice sessions should follow the same basic format for supportive feedback, except it will take more practice and individual direction to master this challenging type of verbal communication. (If workshops are not available for such practice-and-feedback sessions, we suggest having open discussions and practice with family members and actually practicing the delivery of corrective feedback with each other.) And, this is important: While you are directive when giving supportive feedback, you should be *nondirective* when giving corrective feedback, meaning you do more listening than directing.

This may seem counter-intuitive to many parents, who are comfortable giving very direct and blunt criticism or reprimands. In fact, these days a number of parents believe kids in general lack discipline because they are treated more as "friends" or "buddies" by parents than youngsters in need of assertive discipline. We disagree! Regardless of the infraction—the severity of the inappropriate behaviors (e.g., drunk driving, drug use, interpersonal aggression)—the youngster should have an opportunity to explain him/herself, with the parent actively listening with **empathy** before responding, as we now explain.

Ask Questions First

With corrective feedback, you should not come across as telling a child exactly how to do something that is already in his/her behavioral repertoire. Rather, you are merely pointing out specific room for behavioral improvement. You want the receiver of corrective feedback to accept your advice, and this will not happen if your corrective feedback comes across as a top-down demand or mandate without any positivity. Suppose you see an opportunity for a young person to show better behavior in a particular circumstance. What can you say that is consistent with effective AC4P parenting?

Don't direct the child to perform a desirable behavior. Again, this goes against the grain of how many parents handle especially egregious behavior. But evidence from humanistic therapy and counseling informs us that you should first get the child to tell you, in his/her own words, what s/he could have done to be more effective, or to be more responsible when it comes to behaviors such as driving under the influence, using illegal drugs, or engaging in interpersonal aggression. Ask questions with a sincere and empathic demeanor. Avoid at all costs a sarcastic or demeaning tone.

First, point out certain desirable behaviors you noticed; it's important to start with positives—yes, even with egregious cases. "I know this is the first time you've been involved in a drinking and driving episode." "You've been responsible and hardworking in school and have stayed away from drugs until this time." Then, move on to the less desirable behavior. Ask, "Could you have made a better choice in that situation?" Of course, you hope for more than a yes or no response to your question. If that's all you get, you need more precise follow-up questioning.

You might point out a particular situation where the behavior you observed could have been more effective. Ask what that behavior should be. You always learn something by asking questions. If nothing else, you'll hear the rationale behind the undesired or suboptimal behavior. You might uncover a barrier to optimal behavior that you can help the child overcome. Perhaps it is the peer pressure to drink or use drugs. Or, maybe your child is feeling very stressed out. A conversation that entertains ways to remove obstacles that hinder desirable behavior is especially valuable if possibilities become feasible as relevant action plans.

Beyond a Training Session

After you demonstrate with role-playing that you can follow the basics of delivering corrective feedback, if only with your partner or other parents, you are ready to apply your new verbal skills with your child, adolescent, or young adult. Be on the lookout for less-than-optimal behavior and find an opportunity for a private one-on-one conversation. For maximum benefit, the results of these sessions should be documented in Table 4.2 and discussed in class or in group meetings among those participating in this ongoing exercise.

Finally, it's very useful to practice and document occasions of giving feedforward and feedback to people throughout your day. You can practice this with anyone, but be sure to get at least some practice with the children in your life. You should note what went well and not so well when you delivered personal feedback for behavioral support or correction. Reflect on these comments as a type of feedforward to prepare for your next opportunity to improve a child's behavior.

We hope you use Table 4.3 to systematically document your interpersonal feedforward and feedback experiences. Discuss these feedforward and feedback experiences with other parents and caregivers. Such interpersonal communication will be instructive for all as vicarious observational learning (Life Lesson 2).

Parents, guardians, and caregivers: Please know that the best way to learn is to teach; and only through practice and behavioral feedback can we develop a skill. The verbal skill to deliver and receive behavior-based feedback effectively is certainly a crucial skill everyone should develop—from

TABLE 4.2   Documentation of Delivering Corrective Feedback

Undesirable Behavior	Environmental Setting	Alternative Behavior	Recipient's Reaction
1. Left a mess	*Bathroom at home, after morning shower*	*Clean up bathroom after showering*	*Shoulder shrug "sorry," returned to bathroom and cleaned up mess*
2.			
3.			
4.			
5.			

TABLE 4.3   Documentation of Feedforward and Feedback Experiences

Feedforward or Feedback	Target Behavior	Situation or Context	Positive Outcome	Room for Improvement
1. Feedforward: "Please be home tonight by curfew, which is 11:00 p.m."	Home on time	17-year-old son going out with friends	Son agrees, and does return before 11:00 p.m.	Dad gave son supportive feedback the next day
2. Son returns home before curfew	Home on time	17-year-old returns home at 10:45 p.m.	Up waiting for him, Dad commends son for beating the curfew	Dad gave specific supportive feedback, but son seemed to blow it off with "No problem."
3.				
4.				
5.				

childhood to adulthood and beyond to those senior-citizen years. We are clearly never too old to learn interpersonal communication skills.

Specific Childcare Challenges: The Basic Three

At this point we've covered the parenting lessons based on ABS. The next three life lessons connect ABS with select principles from **humanism**, reflecting further the academic foundation of AC4P: humanistic behaviorism. The final three parenting lessons are most relevant for raising and advising older children, from ages 8 to 18, and even into adult stages when parenting often happens from a distance.

Before moving on to these next life lessons, we cover applications of the first four life lessons for effective behavior management of young children with regard to three particular child-rearing challenges. Roger McIntire refers to these as "the basic three": eating, sleeping, and toilet training.[38] Why, because they are so necessary, and to some extent difficult to manage effectively and efficiently.

These behaviors relate to basic bodily functions, which are controlled by internal factors as much as external conditions. Struggling with these behaviors can be especially distressful for caregivers because they seem difficult to control and are necessary for survival. Unfortunately, parental/caregiver distress, annoyance, impatience, and anger can interfere with applying the ABS principles consistently and create a negative atmosphere for the child.

According to McIntire, the basic three are challenging because: (a) they are somewhat out of the caregiver's control, (b) they are relatively difficult for the child to control, (c) the child's *need* for food, sleep, or elimination is not directly observable, (d) relevant behaviors are influenced by many other conditions (e.g., diet, exercise, mood), (e) cultural taboos are linked to these behaviors (e.g., "Your child still wears diapers?!"), and (f) they are somewhat private activities.

The basic three are still influenced by environmental factors, and parents can manage the environment so that it connects with the child's body in ways that set the stage for success. The following sections describe the basic three in the context of ABS, illustrating how to apply key ABS principles reflected in the first four life lessons.

Eating

Eating is the first of the basic three childcare challenges. It can, and does indeed, cause significant frustration among many parents and guardians.[55] Whether the problem is getting a child to try new foods, eat a balanced diet, or stop playing with food, eating behavior can be extremely trying for both caregivers and children. Realize that emotional reactions tend to be learned through classical conditioning. (Remember Ivan Pavlov's slobbering dogs.) Consistent pairings of mealtime with anger, fear, frustration, or anxiety can lead to negative emotional associations with mealtime. This can result in food refusal in the short term and clinical levels of anxiety or disordered eating in the long term.

One reason eating behavior is such a challenge is that parents and caregivers can take steps to improve a child's eating behavior, but the child has ultimate control over whether that broccoli makes it down the hatch. ABS can be used to greatly improve the odds a child will eat what the caregiver wants and when the caregiver wants. It's fundamental for caregivers to manage the variables they *can* control (e.g., home or school environment) and work with or around variables *beyond* their control (e.g., individual food preferences, internal states of hunger or satiation).

The goal of changing *what* a child eats is complicated by the intrinsic or natural consequences of eating a particular food. Foods that taste good or make us feel good are *appetitive*; we seek these and eat them more often. On the other hand, the taste and texture of some foods are *aversive* and we avoid them. Combined with a state of hunger or satiation, these reactions to taste and texture have very powerful effects on eating behavior. Unlike young children, adults can decide rationally to put off the immediate rewards of eating what tastes good for the long-term expectation of a healthy body. However, our country's obesity epidemic illustrates that postponing the soon, certain, positive consequences of tasty food is not easy.

Most children have difficulty making food choices beyond eating what tastes good now. In these cases, applying two strategies can greatly improve the eating behavior of the average child who fusses about eating broccoli, and even the picky eater who refuses to try any new food. In both cases, changing two environmental variables can have a dramatic impact.

Food Availability

In most homes, schools, or daycare settings the parent or caregiver has control over what food is available. McIntire suggests parents have the most control over a child's eating behavior when shopping in a grocery store; they can control what foods are available at home. Simply put, a child can't eat junk food if it isn't in the house. So, the first step in getting a child to eat well is to make

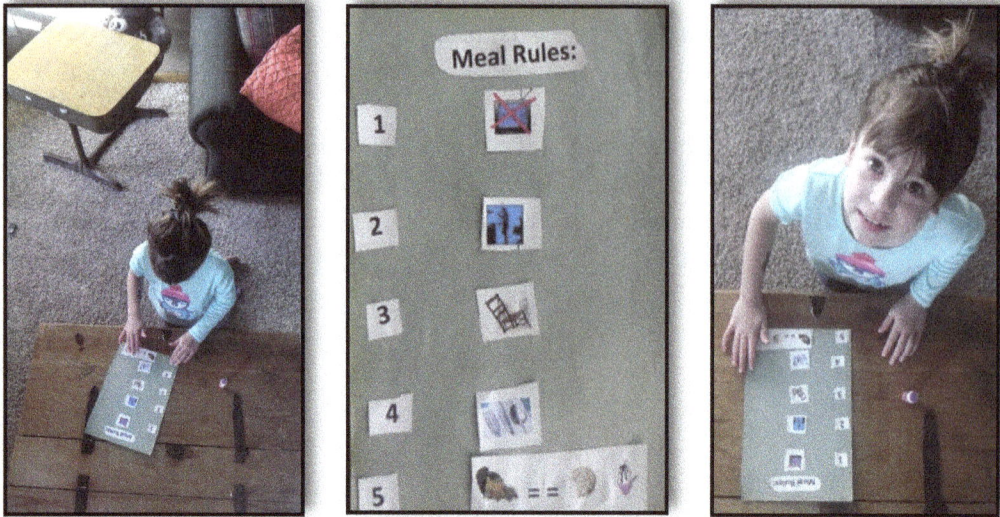

FIGURE 4.8 Prompt used to remind child of the rules at mealtime: (1) No TV, (2) Try it—take at least one bite of everything, (3) Stay in your seat, (4) Use your utensils, (5) If you try your fruits and vegetables, you may have dessert.

sure the available food is healthy. (For current health and nutrition information relevant for children see choosemyplate.gov/kids.)

Scheduling

The eating schedule is a second environmental variable parents and guardians can control. Caregivers cannot make a child hungry, but they can manage the child's schedule in order to stack the odds in their favor. A hungry child is more likely to eat the lunch or dinner served than a child who has filled up on snacks. Keeping a consistent eating schedule, with limited snacks in between, can ensure a child is hungry at mealtime. This is similar to the concept of an **establishing operation**: a behavioral procedure that affects the impact of positive and negative behavioral consequences.[56] Food is more appetitive—even carrots and peas—when the child is hungry.

Prompting and Rewarding Desired Behavior

Finally, the ABC model introduced in Life Lesson 3 can be applied to increase occurrences of appropriate mealtime behavior. We can use activators to inform the child of the expected behaviors. Figure 4.8 illustrates a prompt to remind children of the rules at mealtime. Each rule clearly states the expected behavior.

This chart was used successfully with a 4-year-old. Pictures were used instead of words, as the child was not yet literate. The parents determined the rules, but they gave the child ownership in the process by enabling her to create the chart. The pictures and numbers were printed, and the child cut them out, chose the order, and glued them onto the paper. She also chose where in the dining room the prompt would be posted. This allowed the child to be part of the process, and it became a fun activity for both the parents and the child. Giving the child some control and spending quality time with him/her to make a prompt or behavioral chart can create a positive association with the rules, as well as a feeling of self-motivation (covered in Life Lesson 6).

Sleeping

Many parents have spent sleepless nights battling with their toddler or preschooler over when and where to sleep. Research shows the quality of children's sleep is a strong predictor of parents' sleep, which in turn predicts negative mood, distress, and fatigue.[57] Sleep problems in early childhood are common, affecting 25 to 40% of pediatric patients.[58] As a specific example, one in three children regularly wakes in the night, requiring parental intervention.[59]

These sleep difficulties are behavioral in many cases and subject to ABS strategies rather than a physiological intervention. This section explains the application of ABS principles to common, nonclinical sleep difficulties in early childhood. For information on more serious sleep problems or sleep disorders, see the American Sleep Association's website.[60]

The two most common nonclinical sleep problems parents face with their children are initiating sleep at bedtime and maintaining sleep throughout the night, each problem occurring among 30% of toddlers and preschoolers.[61] The research findings on the positive impact of ABS interventions to treat these problems among young children are clear; overwhelmingly, children show significant improvements in their sleep.[62] As with eating behavior, the proper application of ABS techniques can improve the odds of children sleeping where and when they want.

Extinction of Problem Bedtime Behavior

The combination of a tired child and a tired parent can be the perfect recipe for a child's problem behavior that is actually maintained by parental problem behavior. In general, we are not at our best when we're tired. We get upset more easily and have greater difficulty solving problems in a rational way. Children are more likely to meltdown when tired. So, they are especially ripe for problem behavior when going to bed or waking in the middle of the night.

Typical problems at bedtime include the child's protests against going to bed at a certain time, or the child insists on sleeping with a parent or sibling instead of in his/her own bed. Protests can range from whining and crying to a full-blown tantrum. These protests can also occur at child awakenings during the night.

These undesired behaviors may be inadvertently reinforced (Life Lesson 1) when the child's level of distress seems too severe or the parent is too tired to fight. Reinforcement might take the form of a parent "giving in": delaying bedtime or agreeing to sleep with the child. Sleep protests tend to be intense and get parents' or caregivers' attention. If they happen in the middle of the night, they hit parents when they are most vulnerable.

Whether reading one more story at bedtime, getting out of bed several times to gently tuck a child back in, or having a screaming match with a child who wants to crawl in with you in the middle of the night, you're giving the child attention that can serve to reinforce the maladaptive behavior. In this case, ignoring the undesired behavior is recommended. We're not saying it's easy to ignore a screaming baby or youngster—we've all been there—but this is best in the long run.

In ABS terms, this process is referred to as **extinction**: A response gradually disappears with repeated absence of an expected reward. This is referred to as the "cry-it-out" approach, since ignoring a child's requests or protests often results in crying, at least initially. Both *extinction* (i.e., totally ignoring the child after putting him/her to bed) and *graduated extinction* (i.e., ignoring a child's requests/protests for specified periods of time) are widely used. The latter has come to be known as the "Ferber method," popularized by Richard Ferber's book *Solve Your Child's Sleep Problems.*[63] Research indicates both extinction and graduated extinction are highly effective at eliminating problem behaviors associated with sleep onset and night awakenings.[64]

Why don't all parents use these forms of extinction if they are so effective? Why do sleep problems persist? One reason is a lack of awareness of the proper intervention method. A second is that ignoring a child's negative bedtime behavior can be difficult, particularly after a parent or guardian is awakened from a deep sleep in the middle of the night. Fortunately, environmental and behavior-management techniques can reduce the frequency and the intensity of such disruptive behavior.

Environmental Management for Sleep Hygiene

Like hunger, sleep is an internal state that cannot be directly controlled but is influenced by external factors. Children are more likely to go to sleep and stay asleep when they're tired. We can increase the probability of a child being tired by scheduling bedtimes, wake times, and naps consistent with and appropriate to the child's age and need for sleep. Appropriate and consistent sleep schedules are part of a larger set of recommended practices referred to as *sleep hygiene.*

Sleep hygiene is a set of behaviors that support better quality and quantity of sleep.[65] Recommendations include eliminating caffeine and sugar intake before bedtime, developing a calming bedtime routine, maintaining a consistent bedtime and wake-time process, and avoiding media, exercise, and other stimulating activities before bedtime. Research indicates these behaviors reliably distinguish between healthy sleepers and problem sleepers and they are often a key component in the treatment of sleep disorders. For children, good sleep hygiene is associated with better sleep quantity and quality.[66] From an ABS perspective, consider our sleep hygiene guidelines as empirically-supported recommendations for managing external factors that influence the target behavior: sleep.

Finally, a reward chart can be used to reward desired bedtime behavior (e.g., going to bed without fussing, staying in bed all night). Figure 4.9 illustrates a basic sleep-hygiene reward chart, used with a 4-year-old girl who was having trouble staying in her own bed throughout the night. The chart is designed so that each night the child successfully sleeps in her own bed she earns a sticker, to be placed on a star or moon shape. Once she has earned seven stickers, she earns a trip to the ice cream parlor.

FIGURE 4.9 A sleep-hygiene reward chart.

In summary, ABS provides several tools to promote healthy sleep throughout early childhood. Extinction of undesired behavior, environmental management, and positive consequences can greatly reduce the bedtime brawls and midnight madness all too common among young children. Helping our children develop a healthy sleep routine in early childhood reflects AC4P; it prevents frustration and negative associations with sleep, promotes good health, and sets a foundation for sound sleep throughout the life span.

Toilet Training

Not needing to change diapers is certainly appealing to parents and is a significant accomplishment for children, but getting to this state can be challenging. Popular children's TV programs often feature commercials with children enjoying a celebration with a big parade, flashing lights, confetti, and music after they use the potty successfully. Although the celebration is a positive consequence, busy parents and caregivers with many competing demands cannot produce a parade each time the target behavior is completed. However, busy parents and caregivers can build excitement with clear expectations, verbal praise, and rewards. The AC4P approach provides a solid framework for customizing an intervention for a particular child and setting.

Once the child has begun to show interest (even if just a little) in the process of toilet training, it's important to jump right in. The typical age range is between 22 and 24 months. However, research suggests looking for readiness behaviors of the child instead of relying on age.[67] Such initial interest is shown by: (a) increasingly dry diapers after a nap; (b) children saying they have to go potty; or (c) children imitating potty-relevant behavior.

At the start, spend time identifying what types of positive consequences might serve as a fitting reward for the child.[68] Understanding an individual child's "currency" is critical for success, as not all children are interested in mini M&Ms, coins, or stickers (though these can be very helpful).

For instance, if the target for toilet training is a little boy who finds all things about trains to be exciting, trains become the currency. Perhaps as the process continues, the little boy shows intense interest in fish. Recognizing this shift in interest can be central to continuing to motivate the child with a suitable consequence. The verbal commentary accompanying the reward is critical and can support self-motivation, as indicated earlier. More specifically, use words that support the child's perception of personal competence at toilet use.

Toilet training is a multistep process, and children need appropriate support, patience, and encouragement at each step. Showing interest in the potty or trying out the potty without actually going are behaviors that need a positive consequence just as much as actually completing the task. The **successive approximations** of **behavioral shaping** can be very effective with a toddler: The caregiver provides a positive consequence for each small step toward the target behavior until the desired behavior is completed.

FIGURE 4.10 Incentive-reward contingencies motivate behavior.

Positive recognition of the successive behavioral steps will increase the likelihood of the desired behavior reoccurring, and in toilet training it's all about repetition in order to build personal competence and comfort with the child's body and relevant behavior. For instance, if a parent uses the verbal activator, "Potty time, let's go try" and the child jumps up and runs to the potty, a high-five, "Thanks for trying to go," or a small reward sticker could serve to increase the chance of that behavior happening again.[69]

Also, if a child tells you s/he needs to go or wants to try going potty, an immediate smile followed by "Great! Way to listen to your body" is a positive verbal consequence that rewards an important step in the process (i.e., knowing you need to go and moving toward the target location).

Invest time upfront to generate a list of the behaviors or steps associated with going potty. This helps set clear expectations. Figure 4.11 provides a list of potential *activators* (A), target *behaviors* (B), and *consequences* (C) for toilet training (Life Lesson 3). Be sure to account for the type of potty being used. Does it require a step stool, a child-size seat, or lifting the lid? Be aware of each step so it's easier to give instructions, anticipate the need, and immediately reward the right behavior.

With all of the precursor work completed (i.e., the child is motivated, child-specific currency has been collected/purchased, and verbal praise for key behaviors has been identified), it's time to put the plan into action. Giving a verbal cue as an activator and then rewarding successive approximations toward the target behavior is the foundation, with consistency of action and immediacy of reward being critical.

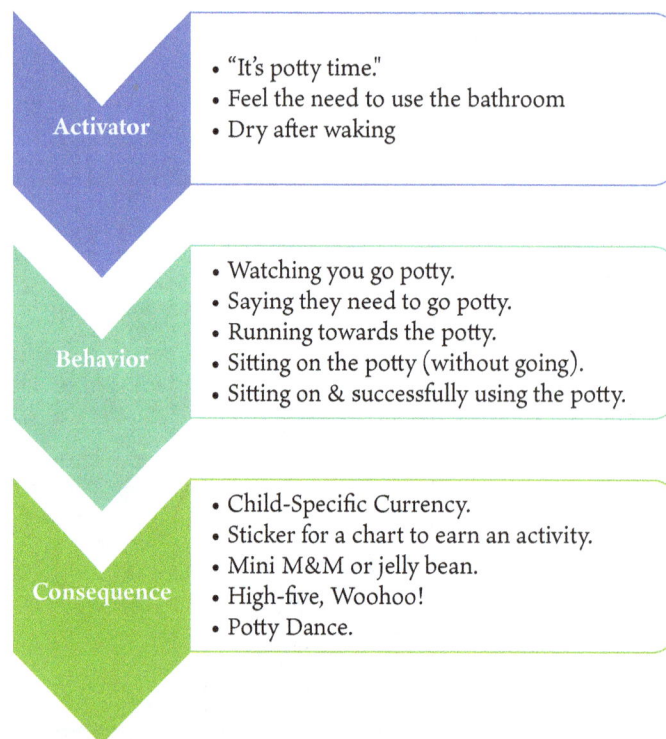

Activator
- "It's potty time."
- Feel the need to use the bathroom
- Dry after waking

Behavior
- Watching you go potty.
- Saying they need to go potty.
- Running towards the potty.
- Sitting on the potty (without going).
- Sitting on & successfully using the potty.

Consequence
- Child-Specific Currency.
- Sticker for a chart to earn an activity.
- Mini M&M or jelly bean.
- High-five, Woohoo!
- Potty Dance.

FIGURE 4.11 Potential ABCs for toilet training.

At the beginning, it's especially important to respond quickly to a signal to go potty and with excitement, even if it's at the worst possible moment (e.g., other kids are crying, you're in the middle of cooking, or you're trying to get out the door in the morning). A missed opportunity to go potty at the right time may result in the child being punished by the yucky feeling of having an "accident." Such consequences may decrease the desire to go on the big-kid potty, especially when mistakes are accompanied by a scolding or a look of disappointment.

"Accidents" will happen; the child is new to the process and working to figure out bodily signals while coordinating clothing manipulation with the potty. Providing a patient and understanding reaction when "accidents" occur is crucial. We actively care for children when we model the appropriate reaction when problems or messes occur. Most children know the "accident" is a behavior they are working to avoid, and they are punished by their own disappointment or soggy undies. A good-natured "Oops, accidents happen. Let's get cleaned up and try again" can go a long way.

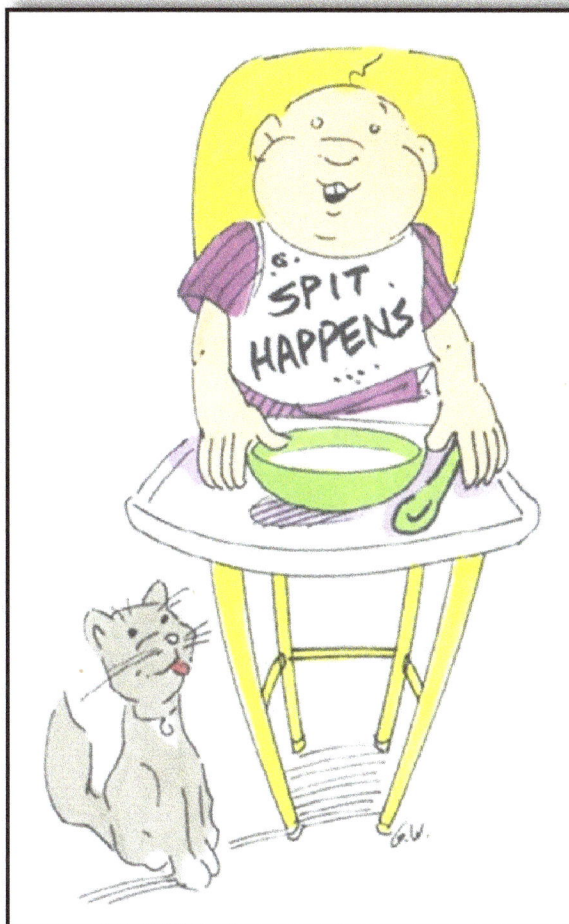

FIGURE 4.12 **We can't control everything.**

One final practical note: An extremely negative consequence for the toilet-use newbie is the flushing of an auto-flushing public toilet while the child is still seated. The experience is overwhelming and unexpected to say the least and could keep the little one from wanting to go potty again in public restrooms. One way to manage this environmental variable is to carry Post-it® notes with you to cover the sensor. Then when the child is finished, remove the paper and allow the toilet to flush. Mastery over the public potty is often the final milestone in toilet training.

Discussion Questions

1. Why is corrective feedback more popular (i.e., used more often) than supportive feedback?

_____

_____

_____

_____

2. Explain with an example what it means to "take supportive feedback to a higher level."

_____

_____

_____

_____

3. How are our "social labels" and "self-labels" similar and different?

_____

_____

_____

_____

4. When is the popular feedback slogan "praise publicly and reprimand privately" ill-advised?

_____

_____

_____

_____

5. List the advantages and disadvantages of using tangible rewards to motivate the occurrence of a child's desirable schoolwork behavior. How might one or more of these disadvantages be stifled or eliminated?

_____

_____

_____

_____

6. Explain a special advantage of receiving secondhand praise or recognition with a real-world example.

_____

_____

_____

_____

7. A common verbal reaction to receiving a "thank you" following AC4P behavior is "no problem." What is a disadvantage of this "no problem" response? What would you suggest as an alternative reply to a "thank you?"

_____

_____

_____

_____

8. Explain the nondirective or humanistic approach to giving corrective feedback with a realistic example.

_____

_____

_____

_____

9. How do the natural or intrinsic consequences of eating make parental control of a child's eating behavior particularly challenging?

_____

_____

_____

_____

10. Explain the concept of "sleep hygiene" with regard to improving the quality and the quantity of a child's sleep.

_____

_____

_____

_____

11. How can toilet training be shaped positively and most efficiently through the shaping principle of successive approximations?

_____

_____

_____

_____

12. Apply the ABC model (activator—behavior—consequence) to one of the three basic challenges of child rearing: eating, sleeping, or toilet training.

_____

_____

_____

_____

Embrace and Practice Empathy

Different feeling states provoked by positive versus negative consequences are the rationale for using more supportive than corrective feedback to improve behavior. The way you implement a behavior-improvement process can increase or decrease feelings of **empowerment**, build or destroy trust, and cultivate or inhibit family teamwork and a sense of interdependent belonging.

Your objective observations of behaviors and subjective evaluations of feeling states should be the basis for your decisions regarding which behavior-improvement process to implement, as well as how to refine existing intervention procedures. *Empathy* matters—no matter the age of your child. You can use it to evaluate the indirect internal person-state impact of an intervention with a young child, or even a young adult experiencing a personal crisis or moment of critical decision. Simply imagine yourself in the other person's situation, and ask yourself, "How would I feel?"

Empathy is not the same as sympathy, although dictionary definitions are similar. *Merriam-Webster Dictionary* defines sympathy as "the capacity for entering into and sharing the feelings or interests of another" (p. 527).[70] Empathy is described as "the capacity for experiencing as one's own the feelings of another" (p. 248).[71]

Likewise, *the American Heritage Dictionary* defines empathy as "identification with and understanding of another's situation, feeling, and motives" (p. 449).[72] In contrast, sympathy is "a feeling or expression of pity or sorrow for the distress of another person" (p. 1231).[73] We sympathize when we *express* concern or understanding for another person's situation; we empathize when we *identify* with another's situation.

An empathic level of awareness and appreciation is not easy to achieve with children of any age. It can be attained only after we minimize those reactive filters that bias our conversations. We must listen intently and proactively. We must hear every word spoken by the other person, while also probing for feelings,

FIGURE 5.1 Mom shows a lack of empathy.

passion, and commitment. These are reflected as much in body language and manner of expression as in the words themselves. The mom in Figure 5.1 is not empathic; she isn't listening from her child's perspective.

When you observe your young child's undesirable behavior, or receive a concerning text message from your middle schooler, or talk to your college student on the phone about a problem, try and view the situation from that individual's perspective. When you hear excuses for inappropriate behavior (e.g., partying instead of studying), try and see yourself in the same predicament. Imagine what defense mechanisms you might use to protect your own ego or self-esteem. And when you consider action plans for improvement, try to view various alternatives through the eyes of the other person. This is particularly important when **actively caring** for your older "children" who are facing possible alternatives with educational opportunities, career choices, or deciding whether to marry or to have kids of their own.

Do you think it's difficult to perceive situations and circumstances through the eyes of another? Are you thinking, "This is easier said than done?" Well, you're probably right. But you're only being asked to take a different perspective into your conversations. Approach your coaching conversations with an empathic mindset. Recognize there's always another side to every story. The other person's perspective might be reasonably different than yours, as reflected in Figure 5.2.

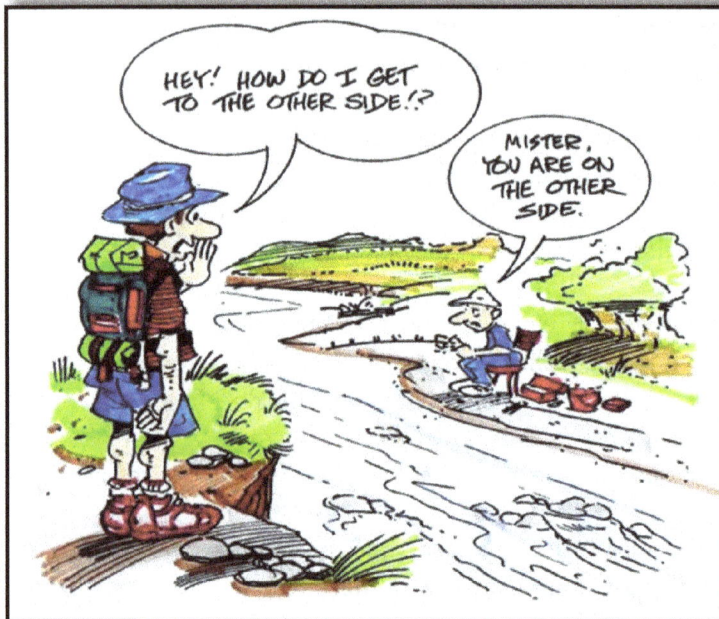

FIGURE 5.2 Perception is personal.

Empathic AC4P Listening

Sometimes parents, teachers, coaches, and work supervisors offer feedforward directions and corrective feedback in a top-down, controlling manner. Why? It's their eagerness to make things happen. It's passion—the drive to make a difference. The result can be an overly directive approach to get others to change their behavior. "Don't marry that lazy slob." "You're not ready to have kids yet." Being indirect or nondirective when giving advice might take longer and be less efficient, but it is usually more effective, especially over the long term. This is a basic tenant of humanistic counseling or therapy. And as your children get older, counseling and therapy become important tools of parenting.

Think about it: How do you respond when someone tells you precisely and in detail what to do? Who is giving you that directive is a factor, but we bet your reaction is not entirely positive. You might follow the instruction, especially if it comes from someone with "power"—the clout to control your consequences. Still, how do you feel? Are you self-motivated to make a lasting change?

Perhaps yes, if you had asked for direction, advice, or feedback. But if you didn't, you might be insulted or embarrassed. Thus, it's better to be nondirective when communicating to affect behavior change. Being nondirective requires **empathic listening**. Again, as children get older and their lives become more complicated, empathic listening skills increase in importance.

Dale Carnegie wrote about the value of empathic listening more than 80 years ago in his classic book *How to Win Friends and Influence People*.[3] His wisdom is reflected in the writing of many authors of popular self-help books, including Stephen Covey's fifth habit of highly effective people, "Seek first to understand, then to be understood."[74]

Carnegie, Covey, and others outlined the same basic strategies for empathic listening. If you've had any training in effective communication, you've heard the same advice. Let's review these guidelines with four easy-to-remember words, each beginning with the letter "R."

This gives you a mnemonic to remember how to listen to the children in your life with an empathic AC4P mindset and teach others to do the same. Today, there is a dire need to teach and use these humanistic guidelines for one-on-one empathic listening. Just consider the ever-increasing "lean and mean" and "win/lose" paradigms of contemporary organizations, as well as our fixation on impersonal emails and text messages, as reflected in Figure 5.3.

FIGURE 5.3 **Digital communication prevents empathy.**

Repeat

This is the easiest technique. Simply mimic or restate what you hear someone (e.g., child or colleague) telling you. This clarifies that you heard correctly, and, most importantly, it prompts the person to continue speaking. After all, the purpose of empathic listening is to motivate the other person to say more so that you can truly come to terms with the issue.

Let's say a friend tells you s/he is very unhappy at school and wants to drop out. The reaction of many parents of that friend would be dramatic and directive, asserting something like, "Oh no you are not! What the *#@* is wrong with you?" We urge humanistic patience and suggest mere repetition, "You want to drop out of school?" You're attentive, interested, and waiting for more information. Reflecting on how drastic the statement sounds, your friend might alter course: "Well, at least I feel like dropping out." Following the repeat technique, you reply, "You mean you feel like dropping out?" Or you might use different words to echo the same meaning. This is the next empathic-listening technique.

Rephrase

Instead of simply mimicking, you might try rephrasing. In our example, you might say, "You mean you don't like school anymore and want to quit?" By expressing the statement in your own words, you show genuine concern and interest in learning more. You're also verifying that you understand. When you rephrase what someone else says correctly, you demonstrate AC4P listening: You have received and interpreted the communication accurately.

Rephrasing also gives the other person a chance to correct a miscommunication, or a misperception on your part. You are seeking an expanded disclosure of the problem. Your friend might clarify, "Well, it's not that I don't like school, it's just that some big kids are always picking on me and I feel scared."

Now you're on to something. Your friend has revealed a more specific explanation and you respond with, "Other students are picking on you?" Or you could *rephrase*: "You mean you're bullied and feel unaccepted and unhappy at school?" Perhaps now you need the next R of empathic listening: *ratification*.

Ratify

Here, you demonstrate affirmation or support for another's statement by confirming that you understand. Your ratifying words demonstrate approval for what is being said. This in turn encourages more explanation. You might assert your approval by saying, "I know the feeling; I was also bullied in school and wanted to quit."

Here, it's tempting to jump in with probing questions to discover more about the unpleasant encounters, the bullies, and the circumstances. Who got you so upset? What did they do? Why do these few bullies make you want to quit? Resist this temptation to direct the conversation. You probably don't know enough about the problem to begin a structured (and unbiased) analysis.

Continued empathic listening might reveal problems beyond the bullying. Perhaps it's not bullying per se, but a particular class or teacher that led your friend to feel so unhappy and/or inadequate, including a perceived loss of confidence, self-efficacy, or personal control.

Let's be clear: A person's distress signals can emanate from many sources, and it takes time for the roots to surface in one-to-one conversation. Plus, if the presumed causes of a problem are disclosed early, it's unlikely you can give optimal advice at that point—directive action that is both useful and accepted. Usually, the best you can do is listen actively with repeat, rephrase, and ratify strategies to flush out the problem. Ultimately, you want your friend to express sincere feelings. This is indicated by the fourth R word.

Reflect

When people reflect on their inner feelings about a predicament, frustration or other situation, they discover the heart of the problem. This self-disclosure of one or more person-states can give insight (for both the speaker and the listener) into the true nature of the problem. Now strategies to intervene present themselves. But even with the outer layers of the onion peeled away, it's usually better to allow the speaker to contemplate a variety of possible interventions.

If you've been patient, sensitive, and emotionally intelligent—an empathic listener—you might receive the ultimate reward. Your friend asks you for specific advice. When you hear questions such as "What do you think I should do?" you have mastered empathic listening. You have shown you actively care. Now your thoughtful direction will be most relevant, understood, and accepted.

A word about long-distance advice or caregiving. Often this occurs over the phone, maybe using video messaging (Skype or FaceTime), or via email or texting. There's nothing preventing you from being empathetic at a distance. You can still employ the same tools of repeating, rephrasing, ratifying, and reflecting.

Summary

Figure 5.4 depicts five levels of listening, with empathic listening at the top. You've likely experienced each of these listening levels as both the speaker and the listener. At the bottom, we've all experienced conversations that go nowhere. We speak and feel ignored—no one's listening. Children often feel ignored. They ask questions or show off accomplishments to adults who are seemingly too busy doing something they believe is more important than listening to a young person. Or perhaps the adult pretends by nodding her/his head, but s/he is really thinking of something else.

Better than pretending, of course, is selective listening. This is probably the most frequent type of listening we experience. It's human nature to

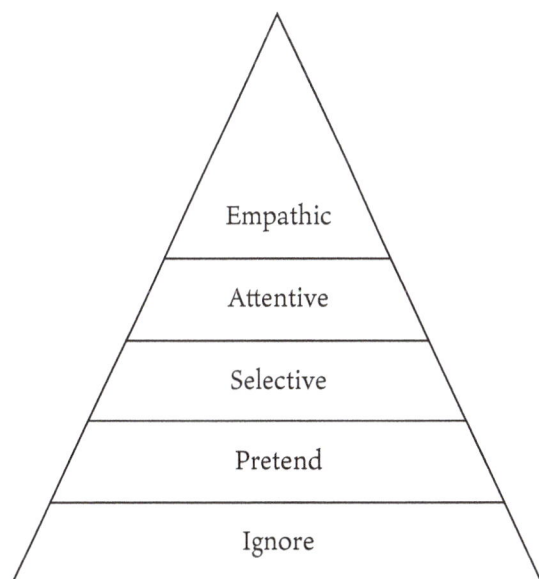

FIGURE 5.4. Five levels of interpersonal listening.

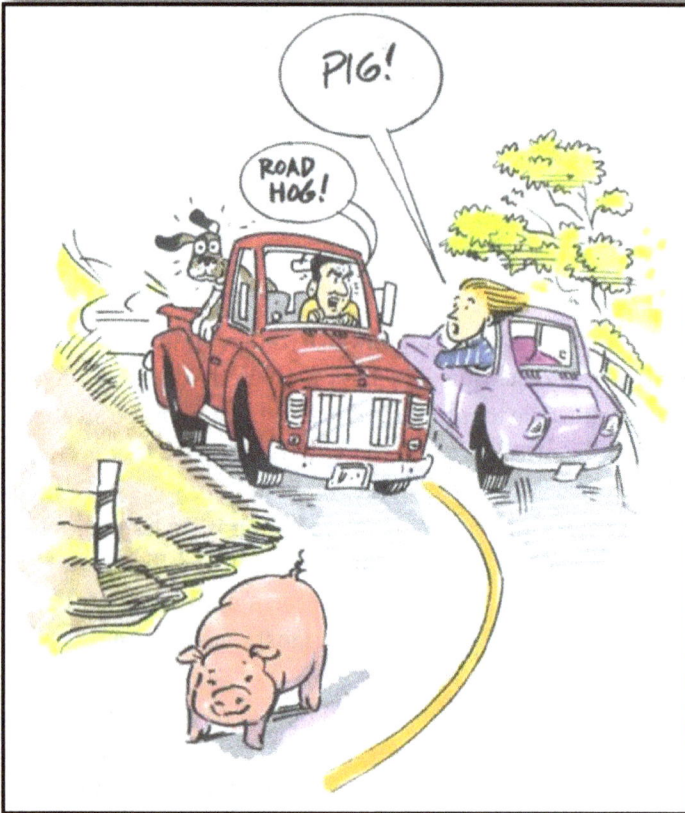

FIGURE 5.5 **Premature cognitive commitment can be risky.**

feel good about a presentation or conversation. We listen most attentively to messages we approve or want to hear, but we often deny or ignore information that does not fit our paradigm or perspective. Psychologists refer to this level of listening as "confirmation bias."[75] We pay attention to information that supports our point of view but discount non-confirming information. We witness this bias whenever we see a Democrat and Republican argue over a political issue or compare political reports on Fox versus CNN News.

This level of listening is analogous to the popular term "selective perception" and is reflected in the Figure 5.5. The female driver is attempting to warn the male driver of an obstacle, but selective perception prevents the listener from hearing correctly. The dog is not biased and perceives the danger.

Attentive listening occurs when we set aside our biases—our premature cognitive commitment[76]—and attempt to hear everything with an open mindset. This is not easy, because it's more efficient and comfortable to listen selectively to information that's consistent with our belief or viewpoint. The top listening level is even more difficult and time consuming. Here, you not only listen without confirmation bias, but you attempt to listen from the other person's perspective.

Patience is obviously required for *empathic* listening, diagnosing, and action planning. Conversations at this level are often lengthy and not time efficient, but they are always most effective. Take the time to question and listen to learn first what it's like to be in the other person's shoes. Your objective then shifts to develop a corrective approach fit for the circumstances as mutually understood by everyone in the conversation. If a commitment to follow through with a specific action plan is reached, you were practicing AC4P parenting or caregiving.

From Principles to Practice

We've reviewed the rationale for empathy and offered guidelines to accomplish empathic listening. You've been educated. You understand the value and purpose of empathic listening. Can you be an effective empathic listener as a friend, parent or caregiver? Of course you can, but it may take some practice, along with relevant behavioral feedback. This is *training*. We suggest the following group exercise:

Divide participants or family members into pairs and ask them to find a relatively quiet location for a brief, quiet conversation. If the size of the group and/or the facility prevents this, simply ask participants to turn to the individual closest to them and execute this practice/feedback session on the spot. When focused on their "private" one-to-one conversations, participants will readily tune out verbal noise from other pairings.

Tell participants this exercise has two trials (if time permits). For the first trial, one member of the pairing serves as the initial speaker; the other will be the empathic listener. For the second trial, the partners switch roles.

For each trial, the speaker tells the listener a personal story, perhaps one related to childcare that could benefit from another person's perspective and/or advice. Emphasize that the speakers will have a maximum of 3 minutes to tell their story, while the listeners practice the four R-word guidelines for empathic listening: repeat, rephrase, ratify, and reflect.

After the 3-minute story, the listeners should take a maximum of 2 minutes to offer their viewpoint and advice (if relevant), while the former speakers play the role of empathic listener. Afterward, each member of the pair should offer behavioral feedback regarding the demonstration of effective versus ineffective listening skills. Start with supportive feedback and then offer some corrective feedback. Your challenge: Practice the recommended ways of giving and receiving supportive and corrective feedback.

Discussion Questions

When considering the nature of feedback to give the listener, ask yourself these questions:

1. How did the listener facilitate continued verbal behavior from the speaker?

2. What did the listener do to enable the speaker to reveal personal aspects of his/her story?

3. Did the speaker ask for advice or did the listener offer advice without a request?

4. Was the advice relevant and/or useful?

5. What particular R-word guidelines for empathic listening were used in this interpersonal communication?

_____

_____

6. What could the listener have done to facilitate more revealing communication from the speaker?

_____

_____

7. How did this exercise help you appreciate the value of empathic listening and perhaps realize the validity of the earlier statement, "This is not easy"?

_____

_____

   The instructor/facilitator should call time after the 3-minute story, and also after the 2-minute reaction by the listener. Then allow 5 minutes of feedback discussion among the pairs. Total time for Trial 1: 10 minutes. If time permits, repeat this entire exercise with the speakers and listeners switching roles (i.e., Trial 2).

   After the pairs complete one or two trials, the instructor should facilitate a group discussion about the takeaways from this exercise. Ask participants to report what they learned about empathic listening from their discussions. What R-word strategies did they notice, and what were the advantages, if any, of practicing these listening techniques?

_____

_____

_____

_____

8. In what ways, if any, did this experience influence your intentions (i.e., feedforward) for subsequent communication with friends and family members? (Note: As you know, when people make a public commitment to improve, the probability of actual improvement increases markedly.)

_____

_____

_____

_____

Manage Behavior and Lead People

6

Managing a family is not the same as leading a family. Parents are sometimes managers; and other times they are leaders. Yes, both management and leadership are critically important to bringing the best out of our children, as well as other family members and our friends and colleagues. Simply put, managers hold us *accountable* to perform desirable behavior and avoid undesirable behavior. Leaders *inspire* us to hold ourselves accountable to do the right thing.

Caregivers *manage* when they control behavior with an external (or extrinsic) accountability intervention or system, as discussed in the first four lessons–founded on ABS. Caregivers *lead* when they cultivate self-motivation by influencing particular person-states (e.g., perceptions, attitudes, and/or emotions) that lead to self-motivation. Self-motivation (or **self-directed behavior**) often leads to **discretionary behavior**: behavior that goes beyond the call of duty.

Self-Motivation

The C words of **choice, competence,** and **community** (i.e., interdependency or **systems thinking**) illustrate the three evidence-based perceptions or person-states that determine self-motivation.[77] Dispositional, interpersonal, and environmental conditions that enhance these three person-states increase one's perception of self-motivation.

Please note that we're talking about perception here. You might think a child is competent at completing a particular task, but that child might not feel competent; the child might not perceive the person-state of competence in him/herself. The same is true with feeling the person-states of choice and a sense of community.

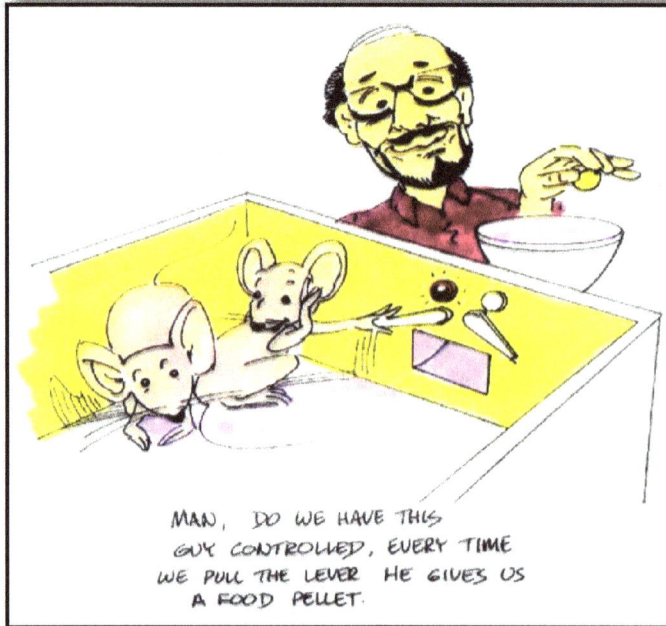

MAN, DO WE HAVE THIS GUY CONTROLLED, EVERY TIME WE PULL THE LEVER HE GIVES US A FOOD PELLET.

FIGURE 6.1 Choice is in the eyes of the beholder.

Perception of Choice

As depicted in Figure 6.1, choice is in the eyes of the beholder. The illustration also reflects the reciprocity of control. Control is rarely one way, although it might seem that way. Students in our psychology classes, for example, exert significant control over our behavior and our attitude through their body language that suggests interest or disinterest. Plus, they can give us feedforward or feedback with a comment after class, an email message, or a personal conversation.

Consider how proper application of the first five life lessons can increase perceptions of competence, choice, and community, and thereby fuel self-motivation. Consider, also, how language can affect each of these perceptions, especially the perception of choice or autonomy.

Watch Your Language

Language can implicate choice or external control. Parents promote a perception of choice when their language suggests minimal external pressure. Phrases such as "Obeying the rules is a condition of being in this family," "There's no excuse for poor grades," and "Bullying is a rite of passage," reduce one's sense of autonomy or perception of personal choice. In contrast, the slogan "Actively caring is a core value of our family" implies personal authenticity, interpersonal relatedness, and human interaction.

The popular phrase "random acts of kindness" doesn't suit the description or promotion of AC4P behavior. Random implies the AC4P behavior happens by chance—beyond an individual's choice or control. A kind act might appear random to the recipient, but it was probably performed intentionally out of pro-social motives. Here's an alternative: "intentional acts of kindness."

Language Makes a Difference

This point is so critical for parents to understand and appreciate. How we prescribe or describe behavior influences our perceptions of its value and relevance to our lives. Language impacts culture, and vice versa. Ponder the words and phrases in Figure 6.2 that relate to the human dynamics of safety, health, or well-being. Do some of the words or phrases on the left suggest negative associations that can stifle a perception of personal choice and/or interdependency (i.e., community)? We suggest alternatives on the right, but you might have better ideas.

It's a good personal or group exercise to consider the ramifications of using these terms and phrases. Adding alternatives to this list is even more beneficial. But understanding the critical

"repeal/reject"	or	"revise/refine"
"requirement"	or	"opportunity"
"peer pressure"	or	"peer support"
"program"	or	"process"
"training"	or	"coaching"
"meeting manager"	or	"meeting facilitator"
"mandate"	or	"expectation"
"compliance"	or	"commitment"
"I've *got* to do this"	or	"I *get* to do this"
"I must meet this deadline"	or	"I choose to achieve another milestone"
"I wake up to my *alarm* clock"	or	"I awaken to my *opportunity* clock"

FIGURE 6.2 Language reflecting varying degrees of personal choice.

relationship between words, attitudes, and voluntary participation is only half the battle. We need to change our verbal habits, and this is easier said than done. Also, the effectiveness of our communication to facilitate voluntary participation depends on more than the words we use. Let's turn to other aspects of our interpersonal conversations that affect behavioral and attitudinal impact.

Participative management in a family environment means family members enjoy personal choice during the planning, execution, and evaluation of their activities—from daily chores to entertainment events. People desire a sense of autonomy, regardless of dispositional and situational factors. But in a family, parents as managers often tell their children what to do rather than involve them in decision making. We come back to the importance of language again. Should parents give "mandates" or set "expectations"? Should they require "compliance" or request "commitment"?

In schools, students are often viewed as passive learners. It's the teachers who plan, execute, and evaluate most aspects of the teaching/learning process. A student's perception of choice is limited. But when students contribute to the selection and/or the presentation of lesson material, you have cooperative teaching/learning—a most effective approach to teaching and learning over the long term.

In the context of families, who sets the house rules or decides on family activities in the evening or over the weekend? What about simple TV viewing? Who decides what show or movies to watch in the family room? Yes, these are rhetorical questions, because you know how particular answers influence perceptions of choice. Do you practice participative management in your household? Do you seek to engage your children in family-related decisions? How are decisions made with regard to what happens during "family time"—from where and what to eat for dinner to the entertainment a family gets to enjoy together?

Involve the Followers

Autonomy or a perception of choice is supported when rules are established by soliciting input from those affected by the regulation. And, family entertainment feels more entertaining when family members participate in the selection of the entertainment or the venue.

Imagine helping a young boy dress in nice clothes you have selected for him to wear on his first day of school. This might feel like top-down control to the boy, and he might resist in order to assert his individuality or personal freedom. Consider an alternative approach: Select two school outfits you would like the boy to wear and let him choose between the two. More than likely, the child will be less resistant because he feels he has some choice in the clothes he wears to school. Little does he know you're happy with either outfit.

Perception of Competence

Several researchers of human motivation have proposed that people naturally enjoy being able to solve problems and successfully complete worthwhile tasks.[78] In their view, people are self-motivated to learn, to explore possibilities, to understand what's going on, and to participate in achieving worthwhile goals. The label for this fundamental human motive is *competence*. "All of us are striving for mastery, for affirmations of our own competence" (p. 66).[79]

Motivation researchers assume the desire for competence is self-initiating and self-rewarding. Behavior followed by consequences that enhance feelings of competence becomes self-directed and often does not need extrinsic or extra rewards to keep it going. Feeling competent at doing something worthwhile motivates continued effort. Of course, parents and caregivers help children view their task as worthwhile. When parents, caregivers, or children feel more successful or competent, their self-motivation increases. As one behavioral scientist put it, "People are not successful because they are motivated; they are motivated because they have been successful" (p. 95).[80]

The Power of Feedback

How do we know we are competent at something? How do we know our competence makes a beneficial difference? You know the answer: behavioral feedback.

As we discussed in Life Lesson 3, feedback about our ongoing behavior tells us how we are doing and enables us to do better. Behavioral feedback is essential to fulfill a basic human need: the need for competence. And helping people satisfy this need increases their self-motivation to perform the relevant behavior. But feedback regarding the *outcome* of a project or process does not necessarily reflect individual choices or competence, and therefore it can be ineffective at enhancing a perception of competence. Only feedback that is behavior focused and customized for the recipient can enhance an individual's perception of personal control and competence and thus bolster self-motivation.

Is Feedback Reinforcing?

Technically, a reinforcer is a behavioral consequence that maintains or increases the frequency of the target behavior it follows. So, if a target behavior does not continue or improve after feedback, the feedback was not a reinforcer. Likewise, praise, extra allowances to children, and letting kids stay up later are not reinforcers when they don't increase the frequency of the behavior they target; and they often don't. However, interpersonal, behavior-based rewards can increase a perception of competence without necessarily increasing the frequency of the recognized behavior. Indeed, the individual might already be performing at peak personal performance.

Can well-delivered supportive or corrective feedback increase our perception of competence and self-motivation? Absolutely, but feedback is not a payoff for doing the right thing. Rather, it's behavior-based information a person can use to feel competent or to learn how to become more competent. There is perhaps no other consequence with greater potential to improve perceived competence, self-motivation, and individual performance than behavior-focused feedback. Behavioral feedback, delivered with an AC4P mindset, is usually a reinforcer because it maintains or increases a certain desired behavior.

Now-That Rewards

At times, special rewards for excellence are given to individuals and groups for excelling at performance in a given domain—from accomplishments in teaching and learning to winning an athletic competition. These extrinsic consequences are well received, often to the applause from an approving audience. Such acknowledgment does wonders to an individual's sense of personal competence, leading to more self-motivation to sustain or even enhance the relevant skill set.

These examples of rewarding desirable behavior reflect a **now-that reward** contingency ("Now that you won the race you have earned a reward") rather than *if-then* ("If you win the race, then you will receive this reward"). Figure 6.3 depicts an **if-then reward** contingency that will certainly motivate a significant increase in service at the restaurant, but the behavior will not reflect personal choice or self-motivation.

Now-that rewards do not include an incentive (i.e., the announcement of the availability of a reward if a designated behavior occurs). The behavior might be initiated for a variety of internal, intrinsic, or extrinsic reasons, but the unannounced now-that reward is given after the behavior occurs in order to support its occurrence. In some cases, this rewarding consequence increases the probability that the desirable behavior will recur. In most cases, a person's sense of competence increases following sincere now-that rewards, thereby fueling self-motivation to continue the rewarded behavior.

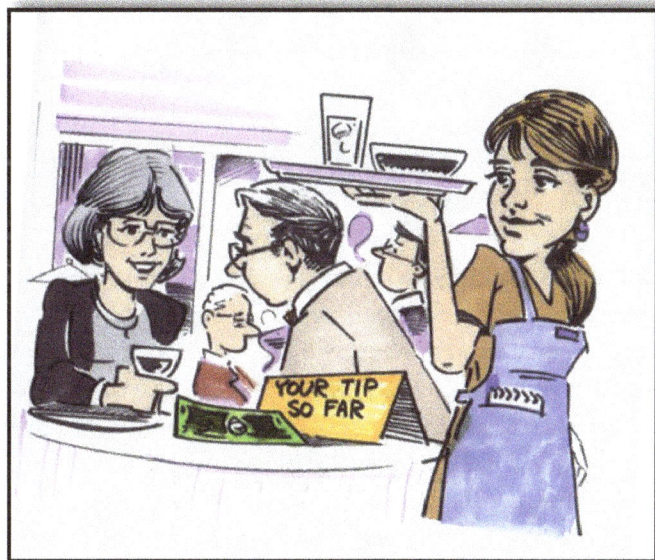

FIGURE 6.3 An if-then reward contingency influences behavior.

A Paradigm Shift

This discussion about feedback, competence, and self-motivation calls for a paradigm shift—a change in the perspective of parenting. We should assume children are naturally self-motivated to do well instead of calling on guilt or sacrifice to get them to perform desirable behavior.

Simply put, children, like adults, dislike feeling incompetent or helpless. They want to learn, to discover, to become more proficient at performing worthwhile tasks. Most seek opportunities to ask questions, to study pertinent material, to spend time with people who know more than they do, and to receive feedback that can increase their competence and subsequent self-motivation.

Consequently, working to be the best we can be as a competent parent or a successful student in elementary, middle, or high school is not a thankless job requiring self-sacrifice, obligation, or selfless altruism. Becoming a more effective caregiver or student provides opportunities to satisfy a basic human need: the need for personal competence.[78] Effective and frequent delivery of behavior-based feedback provides a mechanism for improving the effectiveness of caregiving (among adults) and school work (among children), as well as cultivating feelings of competence and self-motivation throughout a culture.[81]

Perception of Community

You may be asking how "community" relates to parenting. It's all about relatedness, systems thinking, and, in a sense, interdependency. The innate need for relatedness reflects "the need to love and be loved, to care and be cared for … to feel included, to feel related" (p. 88).[82] This surely applies to families, doesn't it? In families we are literally related, but do all family members feel appreciated, included, and cared for? This is analogous to the person-state of belongingness—a person-state influencing one's propensity to actively care for the health, safety, and well-being of others. Geller and Veazie[83] use the term **community** to reflect this person-state because the concept of community is more encompassing than relatedness or belongingness.[84]

A community perspective reflects systems thinking and interdependence beyond the confines of family, social groups, and work teams, as explicated by Peter Block[85] and M. Scott Peck.[86] Community is an AC4P mindset for humankind in general—an interconnectedness with others that transcends political differences and prejudices and profoundly respects and appreciates diversity.

Systems Thinking and Interdependence

Focus your efforts on optimizing the system, W. Edwards Deming tells us in his best sellers on total quality management: *Out of the Crisis* and *The New Economics*.[87] Peter Senge stresses that systems thinking is *The Fifth Discipline*[88] and the key to continuous improvement. And Stephen Covey's discussion of interdependence, win-win contingencies, and synergy in his popular self-help book, *The Seven Habits of Highly Effective People*[89] is founded on systems thinking and a community perspective.

Of course, you can apply systems thinking to your family. A system can be defined as a set of interconnected parts forming a complex whole. Sounds like a family, doesn't it? Indeed, it can be argued that no "system" is more interdependent than the family.

Geller and Veazie propose in *The Courage to Actively Care*[90] that the amount of courage a person needs to intervene on behalf of others decreases as the degree of connectedness between people increases. This certainly applies to family units. The more connected family members feel toward each other, the easier it is to intervene on behalf of a family member's health, safety, or well-being.

Developing a community or interdependent spirit in a family, a classroom, or throughout an organization leads to two primary human performance payoffs: (a) Individuals become more self-motivated to do the right thing, and (b) People are more likely to actively care for the well-being of others. In their reality-based narrative, Geller and Veazie illustrate the dos and don'ts of building an interdependent community perspective.[83]

More Paradigm Shifts

A systems or community approach to improving people's welfare implicates

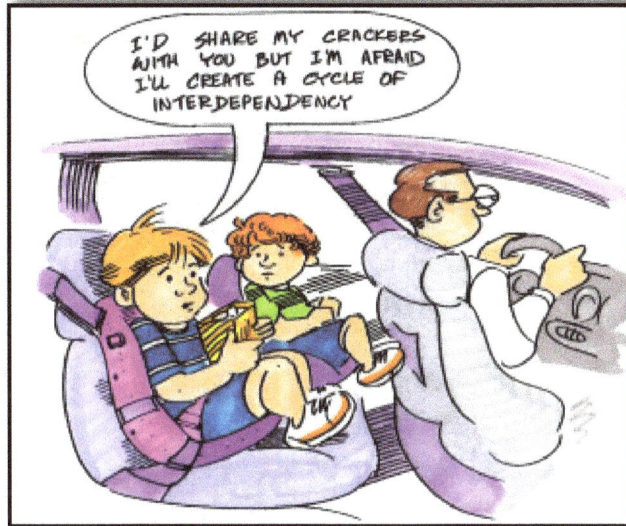

FIGURE 6.4. Teach children the power of interdependence.

a number of paradigm shifts from the traditional management of an organization, a classroom, and, yes, a family. We need to shift from trying to find one root cause of a problem (e.g., the house is chaotic because Tommy is out of control) to considering a number of potential contributing factors from each of three domains: environment, behavior, and person. Interdependent systems thinking requires a shift from downstream outcome-based measures of individual or group performance (grades, injury rates, familial acceptance) to a more proactive and diagnostic evaluation of process variables within the environment, behavior, and person domains.

Systems thinking enables a useful perspective on basic principles of human motivation, attitude formation, and behavior change. The influence of activators and consequences on behavior was presented linearly in Life Lesson 3 (see Figure 3.4). But systems thinking implicates a circular or spiral perspective. While an event preceding a behavior might direct it, and a particular event following a behavior determines whether it will occur again, it's instructive to realize that the consequence of one behavior can serve as the activator of a next behavior. With this perspective, behavior-based feedback can serve as a motivating consequence and/or a directing activator, depending on when and how it's presented.

Spiral causality and the consistency principle combine to explain how small changes in behavior can result in attitude change, followed by more behavior change and then more desired attitude change, leading eventually to personal commitment and total involvement in the process.[91] Similarly, the notion of spiral causality and the reciprocity principle explain why initial AC4P behavior by a few individuals can result in more and more AC4P behavior by many individuals, and eventually an AC4P culture.

This circular or spiraling *ripple effect* can eventually lead to families, classrooms, and community groups performing AC4P behavior regularly on behalf of the health, welfare, and well-being of each other with a win-win interdependent attitude and a proactive mindset. In the end we have AC4P synergy. It can all start with systems thinking or one intentional act of kindness from one person to another.

FIGURE 6.5 Top-down control can stifle empowerment.

Empowerment

In the management literature, empowerment typically refers to delegating authority or responsibility, or to sharing decision making. But when a manager says, "I empower you," s/he usually means, "Get'er done." As reflected in Figure 6.5, the message is, "Make it happen; no questions asked." As we discussed, a parent can be a manager or a leader. When the caregiver practices AC4P leadership, s/he first assesses whether the "empowered" individual feels empowered. "Can you handle the additional assignment?" This assessment of feeling empowered involves asking three questions derived from social learning theory.[92]

As depicted in Figure 6.6, "Can I do it?" asks if the empowered individual or group has the resources, time, knowledge, and ability to handle the assignment. The knowledge and ability components refer to training, and the term *self-efficacy* places the focus on personal belief. We're talking about perception again.

You might think a child or student has the competence to complete a task, but this so-called empowered person might beg to differ. A yes answer to the first empowerment question by those who receive the assignment shows that they believe in their own personal effectiveness. The second question is the **response-efficacy** question. It asks if those who are empowered believe pursuing and accomplishing the assignment or attaining the process goal (i.e., performing the required behaviors) will result in desired consequences.

A sports team answers yes to this question when athletes believe a new workout routine or competition strategy will increase the probability of winning. Yes, it will work. And a student studying for an exam gives a yes answer to response-efficacy if s/he believes the study strategy will contribute to earning a higher exam grade. The long-term behavioral outcome of these two examples can be something more distant and substantive, such as having a winning season or gaining admission into a college or university of choice.

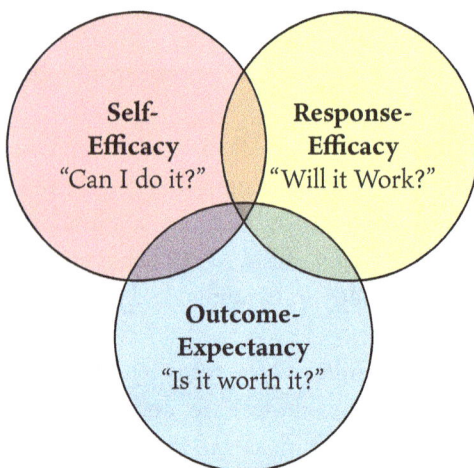

FIGURE 6.6 The three beliefs that determine empowerment.

A no answer to the self-efficacy question indicates a need for more training. Still, people might believe they can accomplish a particular process or task (i.e., they have self-efficacy), but they might not believe this accomplishment makes a difference in a desired outcome or mission (i.e., response efficacy). In this case, education is needed, including an explanation of an evidence-based principle or theory and perhaps a presentation of convincing data. (Recall the distinction between training and education explained in the preface.)

The third empowerment-assessment question reflects motivation. Is the expected outcome worth the effort? Children and college students are always asking this question: Is it worth it? Is it worth cleaning up my room? Is it worth studying for this final exam? Is it worth not texting while driving? The performance of relevant behavior is motivated by anticipating a positive consequence to achieve or a negative consequence to avoid. Refer back to Life Lesson 1 and recall that people feel more choice and are more likely to be self-motivated when they perceive they are trying to achieve a positive consequence, as opposed to avoiding a negative consequence.

Empowering Goals

Behavior-focused **goal setting** facilitates individual and/or group success. It's an activator of process activities aimed at achieving a particular outcome. Perhaps you're aware of a popular acronym used to define the characteristics of an effective goal: SMART. Actually, a few variations exist of the words reflected by these acronym letters, with *M* representing measurable or motivational, and *T* referring to timely or trackable, for example.

We propose these acronym words: *S* for specific, *M* for motivational, *A* for attainable, *R* for relevant, and *T* for trackable, and the addition of an *S* for shared (i.e., SMARTS). We added that last *S* because social support can increase commitment to reaching a goal, and family members, friends, or colleagues who are aware of your goal can provide feedforward and feedback to fuel your self-motivation. Please note the connection between SMARTS goals and the empowerment model discussed.

SMARTS goals empower family members because they are *attainable* ("I can do it"), *motivational* ("It's worth it"), and *relevant* ("It will work"). This connection makes it clear that both empowerment and goal setting are similar behavioral antecedents, setting the stage for or activating certain behavior(s). Each of these activators of behavior defines motivation as anticipating a desired consequence or outcome.

Verbal behavior that contributes to goal setting or feelings of empowerment is considered *feedforward*, as we discussed earlier in Life Lesson 3. But words can also motivate goal-directed behavior when given as a consequence to acknowledge achievement (i.e., feedback).

Empowerment versus Self-Motivation

Although goal setting and empowerment precede the occurrence of behavior (i.e., as activators or feedforward), each reflect the impact of motivational consequences. More specifically, feeling empowered means the individual has answered yes to the motivation question, "Is it worth it?" and is activated to work toward achieving a given goal. If the goal setting was SMARTS, as detailed earlier, consequences are implicated by the *M* for motivational. An individual who is self-motivated

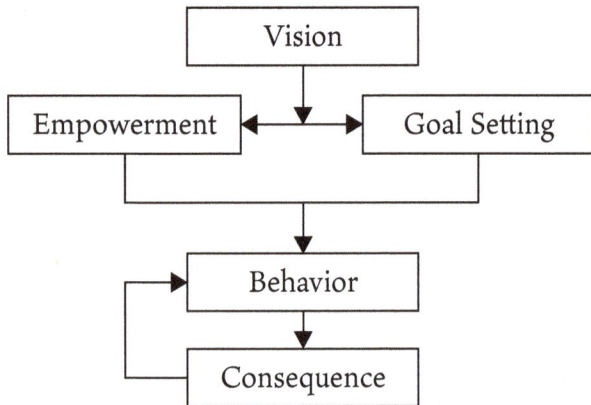

FIGURE 6.7. The connection between goal setting, empowerment, and consequences.

anticipates or has received consequences (e.g., recognition or supportive feedback) from a parent, coach, teacher, work supervisor, or a friend who supports self-directed rather than **other-directed behavior**.

Consequences that reflect personal choice, competence, and/or a sense of social support or community should enhance self-motivation and thereby increase the sustainability of a behavior-change intervention that applies positive consequences (Life Lesson 1). A parental intervention applying positive consequences to increase the occurrence of a target behavior has longer-term impact if it inspires self-motivation by linking behavioral consequences with a perception of choice, competence, and/or community.

Figure 6.7 illustrates how empowerment, vision, and goal setting align with the ABC (activator-behavior-consequence) model discussed earlier in Life Lesson 3. Here's the simple but critical point: A vision and a goal are not enough to sustain desirable behavior. Family members need to feel empowered to work toward achieving a particular goal. This includes anticipating the acquisition of desirable consequences and/or the avoidance of undesirable consequences.

FIGURE 6.8 Activators motivate best when they imply a consequence.

Participants need to buy into and own the vision. They need encouragement from parents, siblings, and peers to attain process goals that support the vision. Family members and friends also need to give supportive and corrective feedback to increase the quantity and improve the quality of behaviors consistent with those vision-relevant goals.

Behavioral consequences are absolutely critical. Empowerment and goal setting can activate desired behavior; but without consequences that are relevant and supportive, the behavior won't last. It will extinguish. In fact, as Figure 6.8 shows, the power of an activator to influence behavior is determined by the consequence implied by the activator or feedforward.

Review and Discussion

At this point, you could review the key components of Life Lesson 6 (self-motivation, empowerment, and goal setting) by watching a 15-minute TEDx Talk on YouTube. Simply Google "Scott Geller TEDx," or use the link www.youtube.com/watch?v=7sxpKhIbr0E.

Afterward, a discussion involving answers to the following questions might be facilitated. Participants could write personal answers to the questions or they could divide into smaller interactive groups and discuss answers among themselves before presenting group reports to the entire group. Or, an instructor could facilitate a constructive discussion of answers to the discussion questions. Alternatively, a family could watch the TEDx Talk and discuss answers to these questions.

Whatever format you choose, your objective is to activate interaction and engagement. Optimal learning for real-life application will occur if you have an opportunity to express your viewpoints and verbalize connections between the self-motivation concepts and your own life experiences.

Discussion Questions

1. Explain the three beliefs that determine empowerment as a person-state, and connect each belief to methods to increase empowerment through training, education, and motivation.

_____

_____

_____

_____

2. Explain the three perceptions (i.e., the three C words) that influence self-motivation and provide examples from personal experience.

_____

_____

_____

_____

3. Explain the meaning of B. F. Skinner's legacy: "**selection by consequences**."

_____

_____

_____

_____

4. Distinguish between a "goal" and a "vision" with a personal example.

_____

_____

_____

_____

5. The ABC model of behavioral science presumes behavior is *directed* by activators (or feedforward) and *motivated* by consequences (e.g., feedback). How can goal setting provide both direction and motivation?

_____

_____

_____

_____

6. Explain the difference between independence and interdependence in terms of optimizing the output of a home, school, or work culture and bringing out the best among all participants.

_____

_____

_____

_____

7. Which of the lessons in this brief talk on self-motivation were most meaningful to you? Please explain why.

_____

_____

_____

_____

8. Life Lesson 6 implies that effective parents and caregivers manage behavior but lead people. What does this distinction mean to you as a parent and/or a caregiver?

_____

_____

_____

_____

Progress from Self-Actualization to Self-Transcendence

The hierarchy of needs proposed by humanist Abraham Maslow is the most popular theory of human motivation in psychological science. A series of universal needs are arranged hierarchically, and it's presumed people—of all ages—don't attempt to satisfy their needs at one stage (or level) until their needs at the lower stages are satisfied.

First, we are motivated to fulfill basic physiological needs. We require food, water, shelter, and sleep for our very survival. Families can provide all four of these essentials. After these needs are met, we want to feel secure and safe from future dangers. When preparing for future physiological needs, we are working proactively to satisfy our need for safety and security. Families are natural harbors for personal safety and security.

Our social-acceptance needs come next. We need to have friends and feel as though we belong. What can be more important than feeling you belong in your family? When our needs are gratified here, our concern shifts to self-esteem. We are motivated to develop self-respect, gain the approval of others, and achieve personal success. AC4P families provide respect, approval, acceptance, and recognition of personal achievements. All of these consequences are crucial to achieving **self-actualization**—the feeling that one has fulfilled his/her capabilities and has achieved one's total potential: "I have become all I was meant to be." Does self-actualization sit at the top of Maslow's Hierarchy of Needs? No, it does not.

The Highest Need Level

Maslow's Hierarchy of Needs is illustrated in Figure 7.1. You'll note self-actualization is not the highest-level need. Maslow revised his renowned hierarchy shortly before his death in 1970, placing **self-transcendence** above

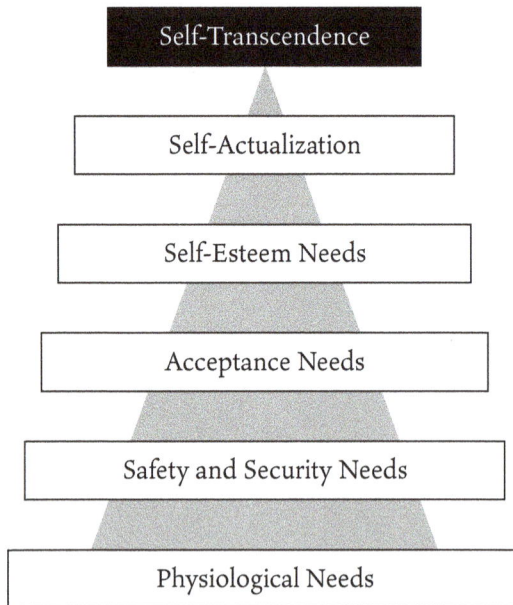

FIGURE 7.1 Maslow's revised hierarchy with self-transcendence at the top.

self-actualization.[93] Transcending the self means you go beyond self-interest to actively care for the health, safety, and/or well-being of others. Isn't this what parents strive for when raising their young? To develop children who will go beyond self-interests and actively care for others? Don't we want to see more "helpies" than "selfies"?

Scant research supports this ranking of human needs in a hierarchy. Intuitively, we might accept that various self-needs require satisfaction before self-transcendent or actively-caring-for-people (AC4P) behavior is likely to occur. But it's possible to think of many individuals performing AC4P behaviors before satisfying all of their personal needs. Mahatma Gandhi put the concerns of others before his own. He was imprisoned, suffered extensive fasts, and eventually was assassinated in his 50-year struggle to help his downtrodden compatriots.

This need hierarchy connects to various rewarding consequences and relates to self-motivation and sustaining the impact of a behavior-improvement intervention. Our position in the hierarchy certainly determines what types of consequences are likely to be most rewarding for us at a particular time; of course, the same is true for children. If we go without food, shelter, or sleep, for example, we'll focus our efforts on satisfying these basics of survival. But after we meet our need for self-preservation, our motivation progresses to satisfy higher-level needs.

Ascending Maslow's hierarchy, we reach need states that implicate consequences linked to self-motivation. For example, consequences that boost our sense of connection with others (i.e., community) satisfy our need for acceptance or social support; consequences that certify our belief that we are competent to perform worthwhile work are associated with the self-esteem and self-actualization needs. Plus, it's intuitive that reaching beyond our own self-needs to help others through AC4P behavior contributes to satisfying our own needs for social acceptance and self-esteem, and even self-actualization.

When is our quest for social acceptance, self-esteem, and self-actualization met? At what point are we satiated on consequences linked to these need states? Indeed, these are rhetorical questions. We pose them to reiterate the value of delivering rewarding consequences that reflect the three "C" words of self-motivation (i.e., competence, choice, and community). These three "C" words reflect need states in Maslow's hierarchy that are most difficult to satiate.

Bottom line: Behavioral consequences (occurring naturally within families) that foster perceptions of our own personal competence, self-worth, interpersonal belongingness, and/or autonomy also facilitate our self-motivation and self-directed behavior. These consequences are likely to have a longer-term impact on us than consequences unrelated to these person-states.

Discussion Questions

It's helpful to discuss practical answers to critical questions implied from Life Lesson 7. Your answers will imply critical takeaways from this life lesson.

1. What kinds of behavioral consequences support or enhance your personal perceptions of choice, competence, and community as a parent, caregiver, or family supporter?

_____

_____

_____

_____

_____

2. In many cases, how supportive feedback is verbally delivered (as discussed earlier) can influence the recipient's self-motivation. Specify the verbal support you have given a family member that connects to the beneficial C words of self-motivation: choice, competence, and community.

_____

_____

_____

_____

_____

3. What supportive feedback have you received regarding your competence as a parent, guardian, caregiver, or friend? What was your reaction?

_____

_____

_____

_____

_____

4. Describe how you could increase a child's perceptions of choice, competence, and community when s/he is learning a new skill.

_____

_____

_____

_____

_____

5. Discuss circumstances that determine whether you are a leader or a manager when interacting with a young child, age 8 or younger.

_____

_____

_____

_____

_____

6. Discuss circumstances that influence whether you are a manager or leader when interacting with a teenager younger than you.

_____

_____

_____

_____

_____

The AC4P Movement

As a parent or caregiver, it is worthwhile for you to understand the background of the **AC4P Movement**—how it started, how it has evolved, and how it is benefiting cultures worldwide. Scott coined the term "actively caring" in 1990 while working with a team of safety leaders at Exxon Chemical in Baytown, Texas. The vision was to create and sustain a brother's/sister's keeper culture in which everyone looks out for each other's safety every day. This requires people to routinely go above and beyond the call of duty on behalf of the health, safety, and well-being of others. The team agreed that **actively caring for people** (AC4P) was an ideal label for this company-wide paradigm shift. Most people do care about the well-being of others, but relatively few *act* on their caring nature. The challenge: to get everyone to *actively care*.

Following the Virginia Tech (VT) tragedy on April 16, 2007, when an armed student took the lives of 32 students and faculty and injured 17 others, the AC4P concept assumed a new focus and prominence for VT students, faculty, and staff. In a time of great uncertainty and reflection on campus, those most affected by the tragedy did not think about themselves but acted to help classmates, friends, and even strangers heal. This collective effort was manifested in an AC4P Movement for culture change (see gellerac4p.com), making the belongingness spirit of the Virginia Tech Hokie community even stronger.

We envisioned spreading this AC4P Movement beyond VT by applying a basic principle of applied behavioral science (ABS)—positive reinforcement. We took the green silicon wristbands engraved with "Actively Caring for People" that Scott had distributed at safety conferences for almost 2 decades and added a numbering system. This enabled computer tracking of the AC4P process: *see*, *thank*, *enter*, and *pass* (**STEP**). The STEP process asks individuals and groups to look for AC4P behavior (i.e., see) and reward such AC4P behavior with a green wristband (i.e., thank).

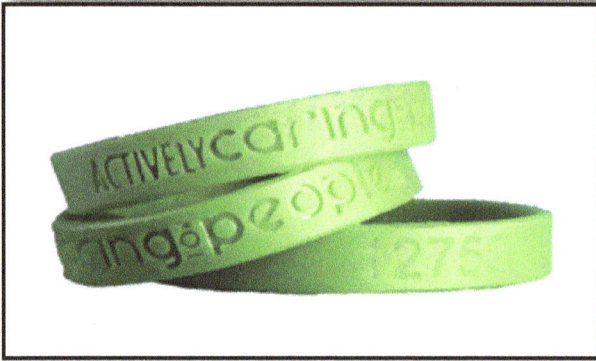

FIGURE A.1 Each AC4P wristband has its own identification number.

The wristband recipient is asked to document (i.e., enter) this exchange (including the nature of the AC4P behavior) at the AC4P website (ac4p.org), along with the wristband number. In this way, recognition and gratitude interactions are tracked worldwide as positive AC4P communication. Afterward, the recipient looks for AC4P behavior from others and passes on the wristband (i.e., pass).

The AC4P and Bullying Prevention

Unfortunately, many parents are confronted with bullying episodes involving their children. Targeted criteria for selecting a bullying-prevention program are provided by Colvin et al.[94] Specifically, they advise the intervention process to (a) be supported by research; (b) be based on behavioral science; and (c) teach the replacement of bullying behavior with prosocial behavior.

But many American schools attempt to curb bullying by turning to rule enforcement and punishment. School psychologists have reported the three most frequently used intervention strategies: (a) discussions between school personnel and bullies after bullying incidents; (b) negative consequences (e.g., suspension) for bullying; and (c) heightened supervision in less structured places (e.g., the playground).[94]

Classroom rules, teacher training, and improved classroom management were identified in a meta-analysis as the most frequently-used program elements.[95] Unfortunately, traditional anti-bullying interventions have a poor history of effectiveness.[96] Additionally, punitive approaches to behavior change have a number of serious short- and long-term disadvantages.[97] A distinctly different and positive approach to bullying prevention is needed.

The ABS components of AC4P parenting detailed in this teaching/learning manual focus on: (a) improving observable behavior; (b) using activators to direct behavior; and (c) applying positive consequences to support behavior.

AC4P parenting also applies: (a) supportive feedback and recognition as positive consequences to reward AC4P behavior, increase perceived competence and fuel self-motivation; (b) evidence-based strategies to enhance perceived empowerment and self-motivation; and (c) interpersonal communication to boost self-esteem, self-efficacy, personal control, optimism, belongingness, and interdependence.

A widely practiced and effective way to eliminate an undesirable behavior is to reward desirable behavior incompatible with the undesirable behavior.[98] For anti-bullying, this translates to rewarding prosocial behavior in lieu of bully-related behavior.

Any action that benefits another person is prosocial behavior, including sharing, helping, cooperating, donating, and volunteering.[99] Research suggests a school-based approach that focuses on modeling and rewarding prosocial behavior has potential as an anti-bullying intervention.

For example, Honig and Pollack demonstrated that one month of daily discussions with second graders sharing their prosocial actions between themselves and others increased the number of prosocial actions observed among students compared to classrooms without these daily discussion sessions.[100] In fact, Demaray and Malecki specifically recommend social support as a program-enhancing component for bullying prevention.[101]

The Anti-Bullying Intervention

To increase prosocial behavior, our intervention process established an *if-then* contingency to motivate AC4P behavior among fourth-, fifth-, and sixth-grade students. To be eligible to wear the **AC4P wristband** for a day, students could (a) write a story about a specific AC4P behavior they observed, or (b) be observed performing an AC4P behavior by another student who documents that behavior.

At the start of each day, the classroom teacher selected three AC4P stories to read aloud to the class, publicly recognizing the students in each story. From these three stories, one story was selected, and the pair of students involved—the good-deed performer and the observer—were each given a green AC4P wristband. These two students wore the AC4P wristband for the entire day, as the "actively-caring heroes of the day." This cycle of sharing AC4P stories and recognizing certain AC4P observers and performers was repeated each day for 5 consecutive weeks.

The teacher's selection of stories to read each day and the one story to use for the wristband reward was not random. During the 5-week intervention, every student was given an opportunity to be recognized at least once as the AC4P observer and once as the AC4P performer. To increase the likelihood the class would meet the team goal of every student participating at least once as both an observer and a performer, the teachers picked stories from students who rarely submitted them.

Each week, from weeks 2 to 6, the teachers facilitated relationship building and belongingness among classmates by randomly pairing students for interpersonal discussions. At these weekly sessions, students discussed one of the following statements or questions: (a) What do you want to be when you grow up?; (b) share a secret talent you have or something you do really well; (c) what is your greatest fear and why?; (d) what do you like most about school and why?; and (e) share something new about yourself.

The purpose of this exchange was to foster new relationships among the students and potentially make interpersonal AC4P behavior easier to perform and observe throughout the 5-week intervention phase. Students were told that everyone would receive their own AC4P wristband at the end of the program if everyone contributed at least one AC4P story and was observed performing at least one AC4P behavior.

Evaluation Plan

An ABS time-series design was implemented, consisting of a baseline phase during week 1, an intervention phase during weeks 2 to 6, and a withdrawal phase at week 7.

Every Friday, students completed the same survey that addressed both the AC4P and bully-related behaviors they had observed, received, and performed that week. Other survey questions assessed personal perceptions and attitudes toward AC4P. Students anonymously completed the surveys and had the choice to answer all, some, or none of the questions. Informed consent was implied by the return of a survey.

Results

The details of this AC4P intervention to prevent bullying behavior at two elementary schools and the remarkable results are presented elsewhere in professional research journals.[102] Here, we provide only a brief overview to demonstrate the extremely positive impact of our first AC4P approach to

FIGURE A.2 The stained-glass window displayed in the school cafeteria.

decrease the frequency of interpersonal bullying behavior and increase students' self-esteem and interpersonal sharing.

After the intervention weeks, every student in all eight classrooms at one elementary school (n = 199 students) and in 16 classrooms at a second elementary school (n = 404 students) submitted at least one AC4P story and performed a minimum of one AC4P behavior, thereby achieving the classroom goal needed for all students to receive and keep an AC4P wristband. For both schools, the frequencies of observed bullying behavior, personal bullying of others, and victimization due to bullying decreased by more than 50%.

Each week, a majority of students in the classrooms did not receive the wristband reward, because a maximum of only 10 students could be recognized weekly. Yet, marked increases in self-esteem occurred every week for each grade. This concomitant increase in students' self-esteem was a positive side effect of the significant weekly decline in bullying for all grades.

At the conclusion of the AC4P intervention in the second elementary school, the principal requested to use the phrase "Actively Caring for People" on a stained-glass window. Figure A.2 depicts the special stained-glass window displayed prominently in the school cafeteria. The sixth-grade students voted for this window as their class gift to the school.

The principal told a news reporter, "I think it struck a chord with our students, and would at any school. Actively Caring for People has become part of our language, part of our school."[103]

Our vision: A brother's/sister's keeper culture in which we all look out for each other's safety, security, and well-being—where people routinely go above and beyond the call of duty for the health, safety, and/or welfare of others. AC4P behavior becomes a social norm.

How can parents, teachers, students, supervisors, line workers, and even police officers nurture interpersonal empathy, compassion, and AC4P behavior? Wearing the AC4P wristband signifies support of the AC4P Movement. When you reward the desirable behavior of another person with an AC4P wristband, you support the AC4P Movement. Then when the AC4P behavior and wristband number is reported at the AC4P website, positive AC4P behavior is recognized, and the AC4P Movement is promoted on social media.

Discussion Questions

1. What are some behaviors you might observe among family members that warrant the reward of an AC4P wristband?

_____

_____

_____

2. What do you say to a family member when rewarding an AC4P behavior with an AC4P wristband?

_____

_____

_____

You should be very specific when defining the desirable AC4P behavior you observe and appreciate. Hand the wristband to the individual as recognition for setting an AC4P example. Give the wristband with words that connect to a higher-level need. Don't suggest or even imply that the wristband is a "pay-off" for AC4P behavior. That's never the reason. The AC4P wristband is a token of appreciation for the "special servant leadership exemplified by the act of kindness observed."

Tell the person s/he is now one of many who have joined the AC4P Movement—a flourishing worldwide effort to cultivate cultures of interpersonal compassion and interdependent AC4P behavior.

Proceed to explain the STEP process—*see*, *thank*, *enter* and *pass*—so the individual is motivated to continue the AC4P process. Tell the person, "If you *see* someone looking out for the welfare of another individual, *thank* and reward this person for the AC4P behavior you observed with an AC4P wristband. You are passing on your AC4P wristband for the kind act you just witnessed." Then ask this wristband recipient and new member of the AC4P Movement to *enter* this positive exchange at the ac4p.org website. Register the number of the wristband and briefly describe the AC4P behavior that led to the receipt of the AC4P wristband.

Finally, ask the individual wristband recipient to *pass* the AC4P wristband to another person s/he observes performing an AC4P behavior. When this wristband is passed on, a new AC4P story is posted on the AC4P website, along with the particular wristband number.

In this way, positive gossip is spread at home, at your school, and throughout the community. Others see that acting beyond one's self-serving interests on behalf of another person is more common than imagined. AC4P storytelling contributes to make AC4P behavior a social norm. It creates and nurtures a culture of interpersonal trust, compassion, and routine AC4P behavior.

For clarification, the STEP process is much easier *said* than *done*. Why? Recognizing and rewarding AC4P behavior is not part of our normal routine, even within our own families, let alone educational institutions, the workplace, and the community. AC4P behavior is just not expected of us, beyond the routine care of young children. We do not normally look for desirable behavior to reward, even though this is the most powerful way to improve behavior (Life Lesson 1). In fact, we commonly deny even a "thank you" given for a kind act with expressions like, "No problem," "Don't worry about it," or "Just doing my job."

Receiving an AC4P wristband from a family member, friend, colleague, or even a stranger should be very rewarding and memorable. Whenever we explain the AC4P concept to others, it's always appreciated; and whenever an AC4P wristband is offered, it's always accepted with a sincere smile and worn with a sense of pride. We know many individuals who wear their AC4P wristband every day and actually resist passing it on.

Imagine receiving an AC4P wristband from a colleague, coach, or teacher who gives a gracious and tactful description of the AC4P behavior that justified this recognition. Rare and unexpected recognition is sure to be accepted with pleasant surprise. In turn, you can tell friends and family about this very positive and unique encounter.

As these positive exchanges among parents, teachers, students, and school administrators accumulate, the media will take note and report the positive news about the AC4P Movement. The AC4P Movement then spreads throughout the community, and various individuals are identified as agents of this research-based approach for promoting acts of kindness—actions that promote an optimal teaching/learning culture and deter interpersonal conflict and bullying.

Feedforward and the STEP Process

The AC4P wristband and STEP process are essentially a feedback process to show appreciation and reward the AC4P behavior of others.

Parents, students, and teachers search out AC4P behavior in various settings. When they observe this behavior, they immediately seize the opportunity to reward the AC4P behavior and solicit another participant for the AC4P Movement. How often do you have an opportunity to actually observe AC4P behavior in situations where it's convenient or at least feasible to deliver an AC4P wristband and the AC4P Movement message?

Many people tell us they do not often observe AC4P behavior. When they do, it's frequently not socially convenient or appropriate to reward that behavior on the spot. In contrast, we find ourselves in situations every day when someone treats us or someone else with an act of kindness. We then conveniently take an AC4P wristband off our wrist and pass it on. But this type of interaction requires time for a personal one-to-one interaction. We're often in an environment (e.g., a university campus) where AC4P behavior is relatively easy to observe, and it's often convenient to reward this behavior with an AC4P wristband. This might not be the case for you.

Here's an alternative approach to distributing AC4P wristbands and promoting the AC4P Movement. Deliver your AC4P wristband as feedforward rather than feedback. Consider giving an AC4P wristband to a family member, a friend, colleague or stranger after you perform an AC4P behavior *for* them.

After an individual thanks you for your AC4P behavior on behalf of his or her learning, safety, security, or well-being, follow up by passing on an AC4P wristband and ask this person to join the AC4P Movement. You might say something like the following:

Thank you for appreciating the positive behaviors performed by me and others in our community. Wouldn't it be nice if all of us performed more acts of kindness on behalf of others? In fact, many individuals in our community have joined an actively caring for people initiative, or the AC4P Movement, to spread positive behavior between people nationwide, and even worldwide. This wristband reflects this Movement, and I hope you will wear it and join us.

Every wristband is engraved with its own ID number. I will record the ID number on the wristband I've given you when I report this AC4P event on the AC4P website. Will you also report my act of kindness, along with the ID number on your wristband? The website address is engraved on the wristband, or you can visit the website directly by logging on to www.ac4p.org.

I hope you will look for opportunities to pass on your wristband, either after you perform an act of kindness for another person or when you see another person help someone else. In the first case, you acknowledge your own act of kindness, as I did with you; in the second scenario, you reward someone for his or her AC4P behavior.

Of course, this is only a suggestion. You might discover another way to express these three key points: (a) Explain why you passed on the AC4P wristband to the beneficiary of your AC4P service; (b) introduce the AC4P Movement and the reporting of AC4P stories at the ac4p.org website, along with the ID number on the wristband; and (c) encourage this new member of the AC4P Movement to pass on the wristband when s/he performs an act of kindness (as feedforward) or when s/he observes an AC4P act from another person (as feedback).

Discussion Question

After explaining this feedforward approach to passing on an AC4P wristband, discuss any perceived benefits of this process, other than having an opportunity to explain the AC4P Movement and pass on an AC4P wristband. How can this feedforward practice generate more AC4P behavior? Jot down some possibilities here, and then discuss various answers among colleagues or workshop participants.

Psychological Impact of Feedforward

Life Lessons 1 and 3 covered the rationale and benefits of rewarding people for their AC4P behavior. Simply put, this feedback can boost self-esteem, personal competence, and a sense of community or belongingness; it increases the likelihood an individual will perform another act of kindness. Plus, you help that person "bask in the reflected glory" of reaching the highest level of Maslow's Hierarchy of Needs: self-transcendence (Life Lesson 7). What about the feedforward method? What is the psychological impact of giving someone an AC4P wristband after you have helped that person? Let's consider the social influence **Principle of Reciprocity**.

Many people feel a need, even an obligation, to pass on a good turn after receiving one from another person, according to much research evidence provided by social psychologists.[104] When possible, the favor is returned to the original benefactor. But when this is impossible, as when a stranger contributes an AC4P behavior, the beneficiary of the kind act can satisfy the need to reciprocate by helping someone else, even a total stranger.

The **reciprocity norm** and related research suggest the AC4P feedforward wristband influences the recipient to perform an AC4P act. As Figure A.3 indicates, the "payback" from this social influence principle is not always positive, and a lengthy time delay may exist between the behavioral exchange.[104]

FIGURE A.3 Reciprocity can be good or bad.

The social influence **Principle of Consistency** is also relevant here.[104] People want their actions and attitudes to be consistent. This research-supported principle indicates it's possible to *act a person into a certain attitude (or way of thinking), and vice versa.* When people perform an act of kindness and/or pass on an AC4P wristband, their positive thoughts and attitudes about the AC4P Movement get a boost.

Every time someone distributes an AC4P wristband as feedforward or as feedback, a deposit is made in this person's emotional bank account for the AC4P Movement. S/he becomes more committed to the AC4P mission of building positive relations and developing a culture of interpersonal compassion.

How can the principle of consistency influence AC4P behaviors and attitudes of someone who receives a feedforward wristband? You know the answer, right? By accepting the wristband and putting it on, the individual performs behaviors that reflect a positive attitude toward the AC4P Movement. If this person later logs on to the AC4P website and reports his/her positive exchange, more behavioral deposits are made to support consistent and positive self-talk, attitudes, and affect toward the AC4P Movement.

Plus, this individual might receive supportive feedback for the website posting, since stories posted on the AC4P website can be forwarded to that individual's Facebook page. Such social support can serve as more feedforward to recognize and encourage more AC4P behavior.

Eventually this continual spiraling of interpersonal feedforward fueling AC4P behavior supported by interpersonal supportive feedback can result in a genuine personal commitment to support the AC4P Movement.

Discussion Questions

The AC4P principles can be realized for real-world application if interactive discussions of the following questions are facilitated, perhaps in small groups and followed by reports to an entire audience.

1. What positive short-term and long-term consequences are likely if college or university students successfully spread the AC4P Movement throughout their campus? Note how answers to this question can motivate individual and group execution of AC4P behavior (Life Lesson 1).

_____

_____

2. What is the value of recording each delivery and receipt of an AC4P wristband?

_____

_____

3. How could family members motivate each other to record their STEP experiences at the AC4P website?

_____

_____

4. How could college/university students, staff, and faculty be motivated to record their STEP experiences at the AC4P website?

_____

_____

5. Where is it easier to promote the STEP process: at home or at school? Why?

_____

_____

6. What factors might hold someone back from initiating and maintaining the STEP process? How can these potential barriers be minimized?

_____

_____

7. What kind of support could facilitate the long-term success of the AC4P Movement at your elementary school, middle school, high school, or college?

_____

_____

8. Is there more to the AC4P Movement than the STEP process? Please explain.

_____

_____

9. What principles and/or procedures covered in this teaching/learning handbook and discussed among your peers were most useful to you?

_____

_____

10. In what ways are the principles applied in the AC4P Movement useful beyond your role as a parent, caregiver, teacher, or student?

_____

_____

11. How might you apply these principles and/or procedures in situations beyond your home/campus?

_____

_____

12. What did you like best about this teaching/learning manual for effective parenting and caregiving?

_____

_____

13. How could we improve this attempt to teach/train positive childcare and promote participation in the AC4P Movement?

_____

_____

Role-Playing Exercise

This final role-playing exercise is most critical. Participants should practice the interpersonal communication steps of delivering an AC4P wristband as both feedforward and feedback and explaining the STEP process.

This can be accomplished in a family by having parents and children play the role of giver and receiver of a feedforward and feedback delivery of an AC4P wristband. Later, volunteers could replay their interactions before the entire group of participants, followed by feedback from the facilitator and other observers.

Or, workshop participants could stay with their discussion groups and develop a role-play demonstration for the entire group. It would be enjoyable and instructive to create a role-play of both wrong and right ways to deliver and receive an AC4P wristband as feedforward and feedback. Of course, family members could perform similar demonstrations of appropriate and inappropriate delivery of feedforward and feedback with an AC4P wristband, accompanied with interpersonal feedback about the role-play.

The purpose: to help participants feel comfortable giving people an AC4P wristband as feedforward and feedback and to explain the STEP process. As mentioned earlier, achieving this level of comfort is challenging, but participation should be motivated by realizing the numerous positive consequences of promoting and supporting the AC4P Movement among family members and at their elementary school, middle school, high school, and college or university.

Conclusion

Congratulations! You have just learned research-based principles and procedures for improving children's and adolescents' behavior, while also increasing positive connections between you, your family members, peers, and even your teachers and coaches.

We sincerely hope you have acquired more than an *understanding* of the seven principles of humanistic behaviorism (the academic term for the foundation of the AC4P Movement). We hope you *believe* in the validity of these research-based principles to improve interpersonal attitudes and behavior related to activating and nourishing an AC4P culture.

Most importantly, we hope you feel *empowered* to begin practicing these life lessons with your family, colleagues, acquaintances beyond family, and eventually strangers. Implementing the feed-forward and feedback techniques with empathy will surely reap observable benefits. Plus, when you reflect on the results of your behavior-focused conversations, you continually improve your skills at using one-to-one conversation to benefit the behavior of others.

When you add the AC4P wristband and the STEP process to your communications with your family, friends, peers, and others you meet, you maximize the positive consequences of each conversation. You will have recruited another participant for the AC4P Movement and helped to nurture an AC4P culture of interpersonal trust, empathy, compassion, and routine acts of kindness.

Our vision: a world of empathy and compassion—nations relying on diplomacy, communities supporting diversity and interdependency, organizations fostering civility and mutual win-win collaboration, schools nurturing social and emotional intelligence, and families cultivating continuous love, encouragement, and a teaching/learning culture.

Personal Stories of AC4P

Actively caring is a sibling helping another sibling on a homework assignment, a son or daughter taking on household chores for an ill parent, a get-well card sent to a friend or even a stranger, a cup of tea and a listening ear, returning found merchandise to its rightful owner, or shoveling a pile of snow from an elderly person's driveway. AC4P means we appreciate people for who they are, rather than what they've achieved. This is certainly true for family members.

Within a family, we want to appreciate each other for who we are, not what material success we've achieved. In fact, overemphasizing the material success of one child vis-a-vis another can lead to family rifts, rivalries, tensions, and distress. When stressors and life's conflicts take the heart out of us, we need to know someone cares about our difficulties and believes in us—especially within our families. And we need to reciprocate and do the same for others.

This basic level of AC4P behavior can make a lasting difference in our lives. It's not about being judgmental, slashing people's self-esteem, and picking over faults. No, the AC4P Movement values the uniqueness of people. It recognizes human potential and plays positively to people's strengths.

Empathy is a prerequisite. We need to perceive and care about the concerns or predicaments of others. When called to act on our caring for others, we must draw on our inner compassion and courage to act.

The following personal stories demonstrate principles and applications of AC4P. They will inspire you to carve out more time to actively care for family, friends, colleagues, and even strangers. Each story illustrates how an AC4P mindset helped to bring out the best in both the giver and the receiver.

The testimonies make an important point: AC4P behavior strengthens the compassion and caring of the person performing an intentional act of kindness. Imagine the AC4P ripple effect if increasing numbers of individuals experience the rewarding, good-feeling consequences of actively caring for others.

Leaping to the self-transcendence state that sits atop Maslow's Hierarchy of Needs satisfies certain lower-level needs, especially our need for self-esteem and belongingness. Self-efficacy, personal control, and optimism are also enhanced through AC4P behavior. Empowerment and self-motivation are fueled by all of these person-states, and vice versa.

Our greatest challenge is to help others feel the rewarding power of AC4P behavior. To do this, we must develop the context and implement contingencies to motivate initial occurrences of AC4P behavior. The positive consequences of the AC4P behavior witnessed and experienced time and again in the personal stories that follow support the premise that AC4P behavior is naturally rewarding and self-sustaining when nurtured within a supportive AC4P culture.

These personal stories were not due to the competence, commitment and courage of one heroic person. Friends, family members, teachers, coworkers, and even strangers provided direction, mentorship, or supportive consequences. Each personal story illustrates how the AC4P principles enable the development of an AC4P culture—a culture of interpersonal compassion at home, at work, at school, and throughout our communities.

The Impact of the AC4P Wristband

My son's elementary school has a wonderful program where the children are able to submit in writing a kind act performed by another classmate. All submissions are evaluated on a daily basis and two children are selected to wear the AC4P wristband for an entire day. All of the teachers and children are aware of the significance of wearing an AC4P wristband.

Last week, my son—Jacob—assisted a child who was hurt on the playground by helping him get to the nurse's office. The injured child submitted Jacob's kind act, and on Friday he became the proud recipient of the green "Actively Caring for People" wristband for the day. At the conclusion of the school day, he couldn't wait to come home and tell me about what had happened. However, he forgot to return the wristband to his teacher, and it came home with him.

Jacob has a younger sister, and she was as proud of him as were his dad and I. Unfortunately, she was playing with the wristband and pulled it to see how far it would stretch, and it broke. Jacob was devastated. Although we have tried to superglue the wristband back together, he was distraught that the one item each child was trying very hard to earn the right to wear was now broken.

The AC4P team sent a replacement wristband to the classroom teacher, and they continued with the process. Jacob's story suggests the AC4P wristband represents more than a reward; rather, it's an esteemed token of appreciation and a symbol of the students' shared vision to cultivate a more compassionate classroom.

A Student's Note to the Principal

A gym teacher met with a student after he bullied another student. They discussed why it was wrong and the student owned up to his behavior, but his next gesture was a pleasant surprise. The student wrote a note to the principal to apologize for his actions. The end of the note said, "I am sorry for what I did; that was not actively caring."

Some people feel guilty when they don't live up to the AC4P mission. At times, we may use guilt and shame interchangeably, but these terms are distinctly different. After performing non-AC4P behavior (i.e., bullying), some might feel guilt, "My behavior was bad," while others feel shame, "I am a bad person." Prior research has shown children with higher scores on guilt also scored higher on prosocial behavior.[105]

The student who apologized via a note to the principal may have recognized the discrepancy between his actual behavior (non-AC4P) and ideal behavior (AC4P). While some may *feel* guilty, the student's response focused on his negative *behavior* being wrong (guilt). He did not label himself a bad person (shame). This reflects the AC4P principle of targeting behavior not the person when giving corrective feedback (Life Lesson 3).

The AC4P Movement established prosocial behavior as an expectation for students, thereby facilitating guilt for a student who failed to live up to the school-wide expectations. In other words, when we perceive our behavior as contrary to our values or ideal self, we feel guilt or cognitive dissonance and usually attempt to resolve this discrepancy by changing our behavior.[106]

A Trip to the Pumpkin Patch

Most students loved the AC4P approach and the process of recognizing each other's classroom behavior with an AC4P wristband. We had a variety of AC4P stories from the students, but few compare to the following story.

We took our elementary students on a field trip to the pumpkin patch a few days before Halloween. After some time, they noticed a college-age student working and spotted a wristband. One student had the courage to ask the worker what words were on the green wristband. "Actively Caring for People," said the worker.

The students were in awe. At that moment, they realized AC4P went beyond them—beyond the school and into the community. AC4P is not just a program in schools, but a Movement spreading beyond Virginia Tech to a pumpkin patch and to communities worldwide.

Aly Neel's Metro Story

After living in DC for some time and riding the Metro during many rush-hour mornings and nights, I have become well aware of the unwritten rule, "You just ride."

On my way home from work one day, I caught the red-line train toward Union Station per usual. A young man, wearing a suit, was sitting inches away from me. He was so close I could almost touch him. I looked up and noticed he seemed very upset—wringing his hands, shaking his head. Unintentionally, I stared at him. I tried but couldn't look away because he looked as if he was on the verge of tears.

I immediately thought, "What can I do?" I knew I had to say something, but I was uncertain how to reach out. We finally made eye contact, and I gave him a smile—the empathic kind I would give a friend whose family member just died. I wanted him to know I was sorry for whatever he was going through. Immediately after our exchange I looked down, sort of embarrassed. I remembered people aren't *supposed* to smile at each other on the Metro!

The Metro slowed down and came to a stop. The guy, still shaken up, stood to get off the train, but then he paused to touch me on my shoulder. He said, "You probably already forgot what you did. It didn't seem like a big deal, but this year has been the worst year of my life. What you just did a second ago, though really small, is probably the most anyone has reached out to me in this past year."

Rolling up his shirtsleeve, he told me, "It represents a pay-it-forward notion." He handed me a green wristband, embossed with the words, "Actively Caring for People." My mouth was agape. I had heard of this AC4P Movement, but I had never received a wristband until now.

AC4P Internet Stories

Stories posted at www.ac4p.org tell of interpersonal exchanges between people giving and receiving AC4P wristbands after specific AC4P behaviors. Wristband recognition occurs for simple gestures such as holding the door for a stranger, and for more complex acts requiring skills, financial stability, and time. These acts occur in various locations, including schools, restaurants, highways, community streets, and stores.

Many stories reflect competence, commitment, and courage. They involve people acting on behalf of family, friends, coworkers, and strangers in both reactive circumstances and in proactive situations.

Some individuals receive a wristband for AC4P behavior in reactive situations, such as standing up for a friend after hearing a racist remark (wristband #407), rebuilding a home after tornadoes devastated Joplin, Missouri (#4766), helping after a sibling's car broke down (#2974), and saving the life of a motorcyclist after a crash (#240).

Others are recognized for *proactive* AC4P behavior such as helping a friend, holding the door for extended periods of time, walking an intoxicated stranger to her home safely, taking care of a sick roommate, and returning a wallet filled with money to the stranger who lost it.

From Random to Intentional Kindness

Every story is unique, with different people, places, and behaviors. However, one thread runs through each act of kindness: *intention*. Perhaps you've heard of "random acts of kindness."[107] This popular slogan implies that acts of kindness "just happen" without planning or forethought. Most compassionate acts of helping others are not random.

Every AC4P good doer reminds us to be mindful and intentional (i.e., reflective thinking[108]) regarding opportunities to actively care. Additionally, these AC4P stories suggest the helpers receive much in return: smiles from strangers and genuine appreciation from friends. They think to themselves, "That could've been worse if I hadn't actively cared" or "I really made my friend's day."

We hope these stories inspire you to recognize others with an AC4P wristband whenever you see an intentional act of caring. Such AC4P behavior will range from small acts of kindness to heroic demonstrations of courage. Your AC4P servant leadership will help cultivate a culture of AC4P compassion worldwide.

The following AC4P stories were selected from over 5,000 stories posted on the AC4P website, which began collecting stories in January 2011. The stories depict instances of individuals going "above and beyond the call of duty"—intervening as a concerned and compassionate bystander on behalf of the health, safety, and/or well-being of someone else.

From an AC4P Wristband to an AC4P Lifestyle

My freshman year I was lucky to have some crazy roommates who truly tested everything about me. At this point, I was a rough and temperamental personality trying to fit my way into the world but struggling to adapt. However, I was given something from Benjamin Caleb George. It was a green wristband with the following words inscribed: "Actively Caring for People." At first, I wore the wristband to make Ben happy (sorry Ben, but hey it's true), but the words started to etch their way into my life. I found myself trying to become better for everyone, including my friends.

It was tough and I can be a dramatic handful at times, but my life became better and I found myself smiling every day. Today, I lost that green wristband—the one that has been with me for 2 years, showing up in every good and bad photo. I didn't notice until I looked down and it was gone.

Its weight and words have truly sunk into my skin and I guess it has done its job. So, I want to thank Ben for giving me something he might not even know would have a huge effect on my life. And for everyone who has been by my side this whole time, I know it isn't easy, and you didn't have to be there, but you did. For that, I thank you. I still have more work to do to better myself, but at least I have a great start. *Wristband #3017*

Nathaniel C., Richmond, VA

A Compassionate Truck Driver

I was on my way back home to Virginia from New York. Long story short, my car broke down. Stuck on the side of the road we called AAA. A tow truck came, with a driver by the name of Taka (Take-a). This man tried everything in his power to get us all the way from Middletown, Delaware, to Virginia Beach, Virginia (some 215 miles) without charging us $500 dollars. He was sticking his neck out to do something for two stranded women that wouldn't benefit him at all. True human compassion! *Wristband #2974*

Jenee E., Middletown, DE

Offering a Seat

I was in Au Bon Pain and saw two girls offer a seat at their table to a blind student during the busy lunch hour. Then, they proceeded to put down their homework and have a conversation with her and refilled her drink when she ran out.

Without acts of kindness like these, I don't know if the student would have ever found a table during the rush hour at Au Bon Pain! I was so ecstatic to be able to give out my first AC4P wristband, especially to somebody who truly went out of her way to make somebody else's day! *Wristband #168*

Elise C., Blacksburg, VA

Students First

I gave an AC4P wristband to Shawn Wells, principal at Bollinger Canyon Elementary School. This is a public school that hosts five intensive special education classrooms for students with autism and other developmental disabilities.

During the past several years, the special education population at Bollinger Canyon has grown quite a bit, and Shawn has continued to build and support a culture that accepts, understands, and invites special education.

Just a few weeks ago, Shawn designated one of the "staff only" bathrooms to be used for an intensive toilet-training program for a 7-year-old student who was not yet potty trained. This student now successfully uses the toilet on a daily basis for the first time in his life. Additionally, his parents no longer need to spend countless dollars purchasing diapers. Shawn attends and actively participates in nearly all of her student's IEPs and makes frequent visits to the special education classrooms to check in on students and ensure she is familiar with their programs.

With such a large population of special education students, this adds quite a bit of work to Shawn's already busy schedule, but she makes it happen, and she always does it smiling. In my work with Shawn, she has always put the needs of her students first. Thank you Shawn for actively caring for your students and their families! *Wristband #129*

Joel V., San Ramon, CA

Coming to the Rescue

My car has had a lot go wrong with it in the past year or so. I never take care of it. The "Check Engine" and "Maint Required" lights have been on for as long as I can remember, and it's been a joke that any day now the thing might explode (not really, I hope).

I let my boyfriend borrow my car one day, and when he returned it my brake light was fixed, the "Check Engine" and "Maint Required" lights were off, there was a brand new cap on my gas tank (I had lost it earlier), my oil had been checked, and fluid had been put in my windshield-wiper thing.

Turns out my boyfriend had taken my car in to get a full list of what was wrong with it (a long list) and wanted to fix everything. But he doesn't know a lot about cars. Turns out Dave came to the rescue! Dave is my boyfriend's roommate. He happens to know a lot about cars and took the extra time to look over and fix the long list of things wrong with it, just because! *Wristband #22549*

Michelle L., Blacksburg, VA

Helping a Missing Child

I was at Great Wolf Lodge when the front desk called to ask if I was missing a child. I said, "No." When I woke up the next morning, I saw a lady with the missing boy.

The missing child had been in the lobby all night with the lady. She got him blankets and held him. I learned she'd been there for 7 hours taking care of that boy. The boy's dad didn't even know when he woke up that his son was gone. I gave my wristband to "the lady of the night," someone who actively cared! *Wristband #1425*

Logan O., Charlotte, NC

A Compassionate Student Patrol

A student safety patrol, Eli, showed compassion to another student who boarded my bus in tears. The student proceeded to fight with her older siblings, one of them being Eli's peer.

Eli handled the situation beyond what is required of a safety patrol. He was able to immediately calm the child and find a resolution to what would have surely escalated into something very distracting for me as the bus driver. It allowed me to carry on instead of waiting for a safe place to pullover. I gave him *Wristband #8215.*

Jennifer S., Great Falls, VA

Recognition in the Worst of Times

This past February there was a shooting at my school: Chardon High School. It's been rough for everyone—some more than others. Like many teenagers, I feel as if I'm fighting the world alone, not sure if what I'm fighting for is even right. I just finished track. I'm not a star runner; I'm actually quite slow, but I do it because I enjoy it. The other faster kids are still in season and still being coached.

Anyway, after the shooting my high school received thousands of cards. They mean more to me than any of the other gifts my high school has received. Sadly, we must take them down "to move on," as I keep being told. It seems as if half the kids in the school already forgot why the cards are there, anyway.

Nevertheless, I feel as if I need to read the cards just so a person's actively caring is not thrown into some box without the slightest thought. I volunteered two times to help take down the cards. Both times I read each one before sorting them into their boxes. I tried not to cry, but there is no shame in getting teary-eyed.

Of course, some of the cards hit home while others made me smile, but in general I feel that after the clean-up I have renewed strength to deal with the confusing mess of feelings.

I can tell myself I did this clean-up for those who wrote the letters, or for the victims of the shooting, or to help the janitor who would have to deal with the thousands of cards, but I did this for me. I wanted to and that's why I did it.

The day I was taking down the cards I was extremely sad. I was thinking how I truly haven't accomplished anything since February. My grades dropped, and track was not a particularly successful season. The worst part is that my relationships with friends and family have become strained. I keep reading the cards, taking the strengths those individuals sent, trying to feel it.

Amazingly my track coach, Bartley, came up behind me one day and said, "You're a good kid, you know that?" I needed to hear those words more than anything. He pulled off his AC4P wristband and gave it to me. I was speechless. This told me I was doing something right. I had always liked and admired him, but this was something more than I ever expected. That was my coach actively caring for me, and I look forward to paying it forward and passing on this *Wristband #47735.*

Megan W., Chardon, OH

A Very Grateful Student and Fellow Hokie

I don't usually post stories, but I thought this one was an awesome testament to the kind of people we have in Blacksburg. I was driving down Southgate toward Airport Drive and hit something in the middle of the road. My tire immediately burst, and I had to pull over. Of course, I had no idea what to do. I got out and called my parents, as if they could help from 4 hours away.

With no answer I was scared and unsure what to do. The first few cars flew by me and then finally an older gentleman offered to help. He immediately started changing the tire and asked me to simply direct traffic. As I was standing in the middle of the four-way intersection a student walked by. He dropped his book bag and rushed over to help me.

After a few minutes of feeling like I was going to be hit in the middle of the intersection, I called the Blacksburg Police Department. In a matter of minutes two officers responded and thanked me for doing the best I could. I had the spare tire in place; the student began describing the "actively caring" campaign and gave the older gentleman one of the green wristbands we have all seen around campus. Until then I didn't know what "paying it forward" really meant. My crazy day turned out to be a story I'll never forget and one I will tell a million times to show people what it really means to be a Hokie. I wouldn't trade this school and town for anything in the world. UT PROSIM, and GO HOKIES. *Wristband #2517*

Kelley C., Blacksburg, VA

Bystander Intervention Stories

AC4P Behavior Saves a Life

I witnessed a man wreck a dirt bike through a glass window. Once I heard the breaking glass, I ran to the scene and saw lacerations on his arm and several on his leg. I knew this was serious when I saw the amount of blood he lost in the 20 or so seconds it took for me to get there. I, along with another Appalachian State University student, used T-shirts to stop the bleeding and make him comfortable until the paramedics arrived. He received more than 200 stitches for all of his wounds. We were told he would have bled out if the bleeding would not have been stopped right away. *Wristband #240*

Riley S., Boone, NC

Corrective Feedback for a Racist Remark

I invited my friend to hang out over at our fraternity house. You might not know right away by looking at him, but he has a white mother and a black father. For most members of the fraternity, this is not an issue.

However, when we were on the porch one of the brothers, unknowing of my friend's ethnicity, begins yelling racist remarks. I immediately confronted the brother in front of guests and other brothers and told him to stop, that his bigotry was unacceptable.

After the fact, I felt guilty to belong to an organization where this kind of racism was present, and I felt incredibly troubled that my guest experienced this at my house. I didn't know the impact of me standing up for my friend until he presented me with this green wristband. At the next chapter meeting we established a rule and judiciary system to handle out-of-line hostile or harassing behavior. *Wristband #10805*

Scott M., Statesboro, GA

Stopping to Help on I-95

It was the day after Christmas on a Sunday morning at 6:00 a.m. I'm a nurse and was driving into Baltimore for work.

I was cruising on I-95 just like every morning and saw a car that appeared stalled in the middle of the interstate about 100 feet ahead. I pulled into the right lane and slowed down. As I approached, I realized this car in the middle of the road was totaled and none of its lights were on. I immediately pulled onto the side of the road and reached into my pocket to pull out my phone to dial 911.

Before I was able to call, a woman squeezed out of the wrecked car and came running to the side of the road where I was, holding her chest. I got out of my car and asked what had happened. She told me her car was hit by another car, causing her to spin, and then a tractor trailer hit her vehicle. Both the other car and tractor trailer drove off, leaving her car smashed in the middle of the road.

I got on the phone with the police while helping to keep her calm and assessing her condition to make sure she was alright. As this was going on, cars were weaving around her car, which was still in the middle of the road. All of a sudden an SUV slams into her car, causing it to go flying to the side of the road about 30 feet from where we were standing. That's when I really realized: This situation is extremely dangerous.

The SUV driver got out and came running to where we were. I helped keep both of them calm, got their medical history, and assessed them for injuries—all before the police and an ambulance finally arrived. As the woman was being loaded into the ambulance, I noticed she too was wearing scrubs and was a nurse on her way to work, just like me.

I just told my brother this story today and when I did, he pulled off his wristband and gave it to me, telling me to share my story and pass on the wristband. So that's what I will do. *Wristband #17630*

Alicia C., Baltimore, MD

Helping a Stranger on the Side of the Road

The other day my car battery died and left me stranded. When I finally got ahold of my mom, she came and tried to jump my battery, which unfortunately fried her car's battery too, leaving us both in a rut.

While my mom started her trek to her nearest friend's house, I waited by our cars. After about 20 minutes of watching cars whiz by, a student from a neighboring district pulled over and asked if I needed any help. Not only did he stay with me as it started to get dark; he also called his dad who happened to be an auto mechanic. His dad selflessly came and fixed both my mother's and my own car.

I gave my wristband for actively caring to the boy for being the one out of the majority who pulled over to help me—a complete stranger. *Wristband #38955*

Abi C., Chagrin Falls, OH

Caring for Victims of a Car Crash

I showed up on the scene of a head-on car crash that happened in front of us. I and several friends got out to help. I went to one of the cars that had some serious damage and found a young girl inside. Both drivers' side doors were stuck shut.

When I went around to the passenger side I discovered her legs were pinned between the seat and steering wheel/dashboard. While another passerby dialed 911, I got her to give me her parents' phone number. I called them to let them know what was going on.

I stayed with her and tried to keep her calm until the paramedics arrived. Later, after some time went by, she got my number from her parents and called me. She said she had a wristband to give me and wanted my address. A little while later I got the wristband in the mail. *Wristband #12548*

Joey B., Chesterfield, VA

Compassion During Times of Hardship

My sister's husband recently passed away after an extended illness. As she completed the difficult task of going through his closet, she wondered what do to with his nearly new (and even some brand new) business and casual clothes. She saw the bus driver for the faith-based school where she teaches and noticed he always wears T-shirts and jeans. She was aware this was because of financial hardship and not a fashion statement. She asked his size and he was the same size as her husband's new clothes.

She gave him all of the clothes that fit him—outfitting him with an entirely new wardrobe. He and his family are so grateful. I've sent the wristband to my sister and I know she'll not only pass it on but continue (as she has) to actively care for people. She is an inspiration to me and all of our family. *Wristband #15260*

Theresa S., Taylor, TX

Strengthening Friendship

I recently passed an AC4P wristband on to one of my friends at Summer Residential Governor's School. A girl I know was giving me a hard time while a bunch of our friends were spending time together. I left the room, clearly upset, to spend the rest of the night in my dorm rather than provoking the girl even more. My friend, agreeing the girl's comments were out of line, came up to spend the rest of the night in my dorm room with me. We talked mostly about other things.

I thought it was incredibly sweet of my friend to go out of her way to cheer me up. By giving her the wristband I let her know she means a lot to me as a friend and I really appreciate her. She got a little teary-eyed (in happiness of course). My first experience giving someone an AC4P wristband was one I will never forget because I grew much closer with that friend as a result. *Wristband #12576*

Melissa D., Radford, VA

What Goes Around Comes Around

I have always been a proponent of *pay it forward,* and when I initially heard of the AC4P Movement, I felt like a younger generation now had to chance to pay it forward and understand the benefits.

My story began last winter at a restaurant. I saw a family who was told by the hostess to stand outside in the cold. I quickly finished my dinner and asked that they be seated at our table. The family was from out of town, visiting their daughter, and was truly appreciative.

Fast forward to this summer. My youngest daughter and I were at a local supermarket. I had forgotten my wallet but had checks. However, since I did not have my license, the clerk told me to put my groceries back. Out from behind in the line, a young female said, "I will pay for her." I thanked her and tried to write her a check, but she would not take it.

Then, a different young female came from the door and ran up to the girl who paid for me. She said, "You are actively caring, here's a wristband for you, pass it on." I screamed with joy and my 7-year-old child smiled. After leaving, I realized the girl who paid for me in the grocery store was Catherine—the same young girl to whom I gave my seat at the restaurant 6 months earlier. Pay it forward! Actively caring for people can become a global movement with your help! Wristband 13717.

Donna W., Blacksburg, VA

From One AC4P Act to Another

A few weeks ago, Dr. Geller came through the door to our university research center, buzzing with excitement. He had just been to his bank and Dalton, one of the bank tellers, told him she had a story she needed to share. She had been at Panera Bread, venting on her cell phone about an unpleasant event. Frustrated, Dalton hung up, after saying, "I'm in Panera now, I'll call you later."

After she ordered, the cashier smiled and told her he'd pay for her meal because she was having a bad day. Grateful that her day had brightened, Dalton prepared to pass on the AC4P wristband she'd received weeks before only to realize she forgot it at home. She explained this to the cashier, saying she wanted to pass him an AC4P wristband. Matt proudly displayed his left wrist, revealing a green AC4P wristband, "It's alright, I already have one." He had received *Wristband #5707* two weeks earlier from Joanne Dean.

Eric C. & Ilana E., Blacksburg, VA

GLOSSARY OF KEY TERMS

ABC (activator-behavior-consequence) The three-term contingency of applied behavioral science (ABS) specifying that stimulus events preceding behavior provide direction, whereas the consequences following behavior provide motivation for the recurrence of that behavior.

Ability label Identifying an individual with an internal disposition, person-state, aptitude, or talent (e.g., a brilliant student, or a natural athlete).

Accountability system An extrinsic contingency or intervention that motivates people to perform certain behavior in order to obtain a positive consequence or avoid a negative consequence.

Activator An environmental event (e.g., feedforward direction from a sign or individual) implemented to influence the occurrence of a particular behavior.

Actively caring Empathy in action (i.e., compassion), reflected by behavior performed on behalf of the safety, health, and/or well-being of one or more other persons.

Actively caring for people (AC4P) The application of behavioral science and select principles from humanism in order to increase the frequency and improve the quality of behavior that benefits human safety, health, and/or welfare; referred to as humanistic behaviorism.

AC4P coaching Interpersonal communication whereby one individual (the mentor) employs principles of humanistic behaviorism to benefit the observed behavior of another individual (the mentee).

AC4P culture An environmental context or setting (e.g., at home, school, or the workplace) where people interact daily on behalf of the safety, health, and well-being of everyone else in the surroundings with a spirit of interdependence and self-transcendence.

AC4P Movement Principle-centered activities of individuals on a mission to increase the large-scale occurrence of AC4P behavior throughout homes, schools, organizations, and communities at large.

AC4P wristband A green silicon wristband engraved with "Actively Caring for People" and used to reward acts of kindness and promote participation in the AC4P Movement.

Applied behavioral science (ABS) The application of research-based principles derived from experimental and applied behavior analysis to increase the occurrence of desirable behaviors and decrease the frequency of undesirable behaviors.

Avoidance behavior Behavior emitted to avoid experiencing the occurrence of an aversive or unpleasant event.

Baseline The first phase of a study to measure the impact of a behavior-focused intervention in which the target behavior is measured in the absence of the intervention.

Behavioral shaping A behavior-change process whereby a positive consequence (a positive reinforcer) is provided for a response that approximates a desired target behavior; but after that approximation occurs for a number of trials, a behavior that more closely approximates the desired target behavior is required for receipt of the reinforcer. Closer and closer approximations of the target behavior are systematically reinforced until the target behavior occurs and is reinforced.

Behavior-based feedback Interpersonal communication following the occurrence of a behavior that informs the performer what s/he did correctly (supportive feedback) and/or incorrectly (corrective feedback).

Belongingness Perceived mutual social support or interdependency with others—friends, family, colleagues, or even strangers.

Caregiver An individual who attends routinely to the physical and psychological well-being of a young child, adolescent, young adult, or senior citizen in contrast to those individuals (e.g., teachers, coaches, police officers, doctors, nurses, and healthcare workers) who support the physical and/or psychological welfare of others of all ages in a designated domain and for specified times.

Choice The perception of having more than one option with regard to accomplishing a particular task or action plan.

Community perspective The perception of having interdependent social or group support regarding the accomplishment of a certain challenge or assignment.

Competence The perception or belief that an individual has the knowledge, skill, and ability to accomplish a certain task effectively.

Consequence An environmental event (positive or negative) that naturally occurs (i.e., intrinsic) following a behavior or is added to the situation (i.e., extrinsic) to influence a certain behavior, which may or may not influence the frequency or form of the preceding behavior.

Contingency An if-then relationship between a particular behavior and a certain consequence. "*If* you do that, *then* you will receive this consequence."

Corrective feedback Behavior-based information given to an individual after observation of an undesirable or less-than-optimal behavior, often manifested in a one-on-one coaching interaction.

Countercontrol The occurrence of a behavior that is contrary to a desired target behavior because the person perceives a loss of personal choice or individual freedom as the result of a top-down rule, disincentive, or *if-then* contingency.

Defensive pessimism A strategy used by failure-avoiders to help them manage their anxiety so they can work productively. They lower their expectations to help prepare themselves for the worst.

Discipline A behavior-based intervention designed to teach and/or motivate an individual to perform a particular target behavior in a certain way; derived from the Latin word *disciplina,* which means "instruction."

Discretionary behavior Desirable behavior that was not required by an extrinsic accountability system, and presumed to be self-directed and self-motivated.

Disincentive An activator or pre-behavioral directive that announces an "if-then" contingency whereby a certain negative consequence will be imposed following a designated undesired behavior.

Education Teaching one or more persons awareness, theory, or procedures related to a certain task or the circumstances related to that task.

Effort label Identifying an individual with a desirable behavior-based characteristic reflecting extraordinary determination or motivation.

Emotion A potent and potentially long-term reaction to a person or situation that can motivate relevant self-directed behavior.

Empathic listening The highest level of interpersonal listening whereby the listener attempts to identify with and understand the speaker's feelings, attitude, motives and behavior, as well as the circumstances that influenced related person-states and observed behavior.

Empathy Attempting to identify with and understand another individual's circumstances that influence his/her attitude, feelings, motives, and behavior.

Empowerment An individual's belief or confidence that s/he can master a particular assignment or accomplish a certain task, determined by answering yes to three questions: Can I do it? Will it work? Is it worth it?

Establishing operation A procedure (e.g., removal of social stimulation), physical-state (e.g., hunger or satiation) or person-state (e.g., high self-esteem, personal-control, or optimism) that activates the occurrence of a self-motivated behavior or influences the behavioral impact of a positive or negative consequence.

Extrinsic A stimulus event external to the individual, considered to be an activator or consequence when applied to influence a target behavior.

Extrinsic stimulus An observable and external environmental event that might direct behavior (as an activator) or motivate the occurrence of a behavior (as a positive or negative consequence).

Failure accepter An individual who has surrendered all possibilities of successfully avoiding a particular negative consequence and submitting to a person-state of helplessness.

Failure avoider An individual who performs a certain behavior in order to avoid a negative consequence.

Feedback Information following the performance of a behavior that might influence the frequency and/or form of that preceding behavior by supporting or correcting it.

Feedforward Information preceding the performance of a behavior (e.g., directions, expectations, mandates) that might activate behavioral occurrence, perhaps influencing the frequency and/or the form of the following behavior.

Goal setting The systematic process of defining a behavior-focused SMARTS goal that is **s**pecific, **m**otivational, **a**ttainable, **r**elevant, **t**rackable, and **s**hared.

Humanism An appreciation of empathy, diversity, compassion, and human dignity—a sincere concern for human welfare and well-being.

Humanistic behaviorism Making evidence-based interventions from applied behavioral science (ABS) more effective by practicing empathy and considering such person-states as self-esteem, self-efficacy, belongingness, personal control, and optimism.

If-then reward An announced availability (i.e., an incentive or disincentive) of a positive (reward) or negative (penalty) consequence following the occurrence of a desirable or undesirable behavior, respectively.

Incentive An announcement (an activator) that specifies the occurrence of a positive consequence (a reward) following the performance of a designated behavior or a desirable outcome of more than one behavior.

Incompetence The perception or belief that an individual lacks the knowledge, skill, and/or ability to perform effectively the behaviors required to complete a certain task.

Independence An individualistic viewpoint or mindset that sets the occasion for self-focused behavior ("I can do this myself") and inhibits other-focused behavior ("I don't need your help").

Interdependence A collectivistic, we-need-each-other viewpoint or mindset that sets the occasion for AC4P behavior—acts performed on behalf of the safety, health, or well-being of others.

Intervention An external or extrinsic program or process implemented to influence the quantity or quality of one or more target behaviors.

Intrinsic A behavioral consequence that occurs naturally and motivates the recurrence of the behavior as a positive reinforcer.

Leadership Inspiring people to be self-motivated to perform one or more goal-directed and discretionary behaviors.

Management Motivating one or more behaviors to occur through an external or extrinsic accountability system (e.g., activator, behavioral feedback, incentive, disincentive, rule, command, interpersonal recognition, or reprimand).

Negative reinforcement A procedure or situation that increases the frequency or improves the form of a behavior by following that behavior with the removal of an undesired consequence—termed a negative reinforcer.

Nondirective approach Empathic listening and questioning occurs to learn another person's perceptions and circumstances before advice or direction is offered.

Now-that reward An extrinsic positive consequence (e.g., reward, recognition, supportive feedback) delivered following a desired behavior or the outcome of more than one behavior.

Observational learning Learning how to perform one or more behaviors by watching one or more individuals perform the behavior(s).

Optimism An expectation that the consequences of one or more behaviors will be positive—the challenge will be met successfully.

Other-directed behavior Behavior that occurs as a result of an extrinsic or external intervention, such as an incentive that promises a reward following a target behavior or a disincentive that warns the levy of a penalty if a certain undesirable behavior occurs.

Outcome expectancy An individual's belief or confidence that the anticipated consequences following the performance of one or more goal-directed behaviors is worth the effort expended and the time involved to achieve the desired outcome.

Participative management Empowering people to help design and/or implement the contingencies or the accountability system that controls one or more of their own behaviors.

Penalty A negative consequence following one or more behaviors that may or may not influence subsequent performance of the preceding behavior(s).

Personal control One's perception of personal ability or competence to accomplish a particular task or handle a certain challenge.

Person-state A personal disposition (e.g., expectancy, attitude, or personality factor) that influences an individual's behavior.

Pessimism An expectation that a particular behavior or a certain action plan will not be successful or will result in a negative consequence, thereby reflecting Murphy's law: "If anything can go wrong, it will."

Positive reinforcement A procedure or situation that increases the frequency or improves the form of a behavior by following that behavior with a desirable consequence—termed a positive reinforcer.

Premack Principle Increasing the frequency of a desirable, lower-frequency behavior (e.g., working on school homework) by making the occurrence of a more fun, higher-frequency behavior (e.g., playing with friends) contingent on the occurrence of the lower-frequency, less fun behavior.

Principle of Consistency The research-based dynamic that people will alter their attitudes, beliefs, and perceptions to be consistent with their behavior, and vice versa.

Principle of Reciprocity A research-based social norm supporting the notion of "payback" or "pay it forward"—an obligation to return a good turn (a favor) or a bad turn (a negative interaction).

Proactive An intervention process or procedure that occurs before a possible negative event in order to prevent the occurrence of that event.

Process-oriented feedback Behavior-focused feedback (supportive or corrective) that is offered during or immediately after the performance of behaviors relevant to the completion of a goal-oriented task or assignment.

Psychological reactance The perception of a loss of personal choice or freedom due to a top-down rule, disincentive, or *if-then* contingency that activates the performance of behavior contrary to the desired behavior targeted by the rule, disincentive, or if-then contingency.

Punisher A negative consequence following a designated behavior that reduces the occurrence of that behavior.

Punishment A behavior-focused intervention that successfully reduces the frequency of a target behavior by following that behavior with a negative consequence.

Reactive An intervention process or procedure that occurs after the occurrence of a negative or hurtful event in order to help people cope with or heal from that undesirable incident.

Reciprocity norm The social norm that obligates people to repay others with the form of behavior (positive or negative) they had received from them.

Response-efficacy An individual's belief or confidence that performing one or more goal-directed behaviors will contribute to achieving a desirable outcome or long-term mission.

Reward A positive consequence following a designated behavior or an outcome of more than one behavior that may or may not influence subsequent performance.

Reward contingency The process of attempting to motivate the occurrence of one or more desirable behaviors by promising a positive consequence following the occurrence of the target behavior(s).

STEP The four-step process for delivering an AC4P wristband to reward AC4P behavior and promote the AC4P Movement: *see* an AC4P behavior, *thank* the person for the AC4P behavior, ask the wristband recipient to *enter* the positive AC4P interaction at the www.ac4p.org website, and then *pass* on the wristband to reward another person's AC4P behavior.

Selection by consequences B.F. Skinner's legacy that emulates the motivational principle that people do what they do to gain a positive consequence or to avoid or escape a negative consequence.

Self-accountability Internal motivation (from within) to perform one or more behaviors.

Self-actualization The top of Maslow's *initial* Hierarchy of Needs at which a person feels a sense of ultimate achievement—having fulfilled one's self-defined potential.

Self-directed behavior Self-motivated behavior that is not activated or motivated by an external or extrinsic intervention (e.g., an incentive or disincentive).

Self-efficacy An individual's belief or confidence that s/he has the knowledge, skill, and ability to perform the goal-directed behavior(s) needed to accomplish a certain task.

Self-esteem A general or overall feeling of self-worth that influences one's propensity to perform AC4P behavior.

Self-handicapping A cognitive strategy by which people avoid performing effortful desirable behavior(s) in the hope of keeping potential failure from lowering their self-esteem.

Self-label A positive attribution or character trait a person assigns to him/herself from personal experience that results in desirable behavior consistent with the label.

Self-motivation A person-state that reflects internal drive to perform certain behavior(s) or achieve a particular outcome of one or more behaviors from a self-directed mindset.

Self-transcendence The top of Maslow's *revised* Hierarchy of Needs whereby an AC4P mindset is realized, and the individual experiences personal fulfilment and intrinsic reinforcement when performing AC4P behavior—behavior contributing to the safety, health, or welfare of one or more persons.

SMARTS goal A behavior-focused achievement objective defined by making it **s**pecific, **m**otivational, **a**ttainable, **r**elevant, **t**rackable, and **s**hared.

Social label An attribute or character trait assigned to an individual by others that can be positive and thereby activate desirable behavior consistent with the label, or it can be negative and thereby influence undesirable behavior consistent with the other-directed attribute.

Success seeker An individual who performs one or more behaviors in order to earn a positive consequence, which can be intrinsic or extrinsic.

Successive approximations Behaviors in a behavioral-shaping process that come closer and closer to the form and/or frequency of a desired target behavior.

Synergy Interdependent participation in a goal-directed activity that results in greater achievement than would be possible if all participants worked independently toward the same goal.

Systems thinking A collectivistic mindset or perspective that takes a wider look at an achievement, challenge, or problem and considers mutual interdependent and interpersonal influence and ownership, as opposed to individualism, which gives precedence to individual initiative and choice over group or community interest and contribution.

Timeout A punishment procedure whereby a young child is removed from a pleasant environment following his or her undesired behavior, resulting in a decrease in the frequency of the undesirable behavior.

Training Providing behavior-based direction or feedback regarding the performance of one or more specified behaviors relevant to achieving a designated outcome.

Vicarious punishment Observational learning whereby the negative consequence given to one or more persons following an undesirable behavior influences an observer of this interaction to decrease his/her performance of that behavior.

Vicarious reinforcement Observational learning whereby the positive consequence given to one or more persons following a desirable behavior influences an observer of this interaction to increase the frequency or improve the quality of his/her performance of that behavior.

Vision A long-term or ultimate objective or outcome achieved through serial goal getting and the successive accomplishment of those behavior-based goals.

REFERENCE NOTES

1. Geller, E. S. (2017). *Actively caring for people in schools: How to cultivate a culture of compassion.* Morgan James Publishers; Geller, E. S. (2018). *Life lessons from psychological science: How to bring the best out of yourself and others.* Hayden-McNeil; Geller, E. S., & Geller, K. S. (2017). *Actively caring for people's safety: How to cultivate a brother's/sister's keeper's work culture.* American Society of Safety Professionals; Geller, E. S., & Kipper, B. (2017). *Actively caring for people policing: Building positive police/citizen relations.* Morgan James.

2. Fournier, A. K., Will, K. E., & Larson, K. (2016). Actively caring for our children. In E. S. Geller (Ed.), *Applied psychology: Actively caring for people* (pp. 469–505). Cambridge University Press.

3. Carnegie, D. (1936). *How to win friends and influence people* (1981 ed.). Simon and Schuster.

4. Piaget, J. (1952). *The origins of intelligence in children.* International Universities Press.

5. Covington, M.V. (1992). *Making the grade: A self-worth perspective on motivation and school reform.* Cambridge University Press; Martin, A. J., & Marsh, H. W. (2003). Fear of failure: Friend or foe? *Australian Psychologist, 38*(1), 31–38.

6. Ross, L. (1977). The intuitive psychologist and his shortcomings: Distortions in the attribution process. In L. Berkowitz (Ed.), *Advances in experimental social psychology* (pp. 173–220). Academic Press.

7. Damon, W., & Lerner, R. M. (Eds.). (2006). *Handbook of child psychology* (6th ed.). Wiley.

8. Robert Wood Johnson Foundation. (2013, December). *Return on investments in public health: Saving lives and money.* Policy Highlight Brief.

9. Skinner, B. F. (1971). *Beyond freedom and dignity.* Alfred Knopf.

10. Brehm, J. W. (1966). *A theory of psychological reactance.* Academic Press.

11. Knox, M. (2010). On hitting children: A review of corporal punishment in the United States. *Journal of Pediatric Health Care, 24*(2), 103–107.

12. American Academy of Pediatrics (2018, November 5). *Where we stand: Spanking.* http://www. healthychildren.org/English/family-life/family-dynamics/communication-discipline/Pages/ Where-We-Stand-Spanking.aspx

13. Gershoff, E. T. (2002). Corporal punishment by parents and associate child behaviors and experiences: A meta-analytic and theoretical review. *Psychological Bulletin, 128*(4), 539–579; Knox, M. (2010). On hitting children: A review of corporal punishment in the United States. *Journal of Pediatric Health Care, 24*(2), 103–107.

14. Afifi, T. O., Mota, N. P., Dasiewicz, P., MacMillan, H. L., & Sareen, J. (2012). Physical punishment and mental disorders: Results from a nationally representative U.S. sample. *Pediatrics, 130*(2), 1–11.

15. Norem, J. K., & Cantor, N. (1986). Harnessing anxiety as motivation. *Journal of Personality and Social Psychology, 51*(6), 1208–1217. http://doi.org/10.1037/0022-3514.51.6.1208

16. Jones, E. E., & Berglas, S. (1978). Control of attributions about the self through self-handicapping strategies: The appeal of alcohol and the role of underachievement. *Personality and Social Psychology Bulletin, 4,* 200–206. https://doi.org/10.1177/014616727800400205

17. Kohn, A. (1993). *Punished by rewards: The trouble with gold stars, incentive plans, A's, praise, and other bribes.* Houghton Mifflin.

18. Kohn, A. (2001). Five reasons to stop saying "Good Job!" *Young Children, 56*(5), 24–30.

19. Dweck, C. S. (2006). *Mindset: The new psychology of success.* Ballantine.

20. Ibid., 71.

21. Ibid., 72.

22. Ibid., 73.

23. Strain, P. S., & Joseph, G. E. (2004). A not so good job with "Good job": A response to Kohn 2001. *Journal of Positive Behavior Interventions, 6*(1), 55–59.

24. Kratochwill, T. R., & Stoiber, K. C. (2000). Empirically supported interventions and school psychology. *School Psychology Quarterly, 15*(2), 233–253; Timm, M. A., Strain, P. S., & Eller, P. H. (1979). Effects of systematic, response-dependent fading and thinning procedures on the maintenance of child-child interaction. *Journal of Applied Behavior Analysis, 12*(2), 308.

25. Premack, D. (1959). Toward empirical behavior laws: I. Positive reinforcement. *Psychological Review, 66*(4), 219–233. https://doi.org/10.1037/h0040891

26. Stipek, D. J., & Hoffman, J. M. (1980). Development of children's performance-related judgments. *Child Development, 51,* 912–914.

27. Geller, E. S. (2014) (Ed.). *Actively caring for people: Cultivating a culture of compassion* (5th ed.). Make-A-Difference, LLC.; Gershoff, E. T. (2002). Corporal punishment by parents and associated child behaviors and experiences: A meta-analytic and theoretical review. *Psychological Bulletin, 128*(4), 539–579; Gershoff, E. T. (2013). Spanking and child development: We know enough now to stop hitting our children. *Child Development Perspectives, 7*(3), 133–137.

28. Barkley, R. (2013). *Defiant children: A clinician's manual for assessment and parent training* (3rd ed.). Guilford; MacKenzie, M. J., Nicklas, E., Brooks-Gunn, J., & Waldfogel, J. (2014). Spanking and children's externalizing behavior across the first decade of life: Evidence for a transactional process. *Journal of Youth and Adolescence, 44*(3), 658–659.

29. Barkley, R. A. (2013). *Your defiant child: Eight steps to better behavior* (2nd ed). Guilford.

30. Barkley, R. A. (1997). *Defiant children: A clinician's manual for assessment and parent training* (3rd ed.). Guilford.

31. Bandura, A. (1969). *Principles of behavior modification.* Holt, Reinhold & Winston

32. Griffin, C., & Al-Talib, N. I. (1994). Labeling effect on adolescents' self-concept. *International Journal of Offender Therapy and Comparative Criminology, 38*(1), 47–57.

33. Kraut, R. E. (1973). Effects of social labeling on giving to charity. *Journal of Experimental Social Psychology, 9*(6), 551–562.

34. Tannenbaum, F. (1983). *Crime and community.* Columbia University Press.

35. Rosenthal, R., & Jacobson, L. (1992). *Pygmalion in the classroom: Teacher expectation and pupils' intellectual development* (expanded ed.) Irvington.

36. Merton, R. K. (1948). The self-fulfilling prophecy. *Antioch Review, 8*(2), 193–210, 195. https://doi.org/10.2307/4609267

37. Peters, R. (1998). *It's never too soon: A low-stress program that shows parents how to teach good behavior.* Golden Books.

38. McIntire, R. (2012). *What every parent should know about raising children.* Summit Crossroads.

39. Damon, W., & Learner, R.M. (Eds.) (2006). *Handbook of child psychology* (6th ed.). Wiley.

40. American Psychiatric Association (2013). *Diagnostic and statistical manual of mental disorders* (5th ed.). *DSM-5.* American Psychiatric Association.

41. Axelrod, S., McElrath, K. K., & Wine, B. (2012). Applied behavior analysis: Autism and beyond. *Behavioral Interventions, 27*(1), 1–15.

42. Lord, C., Risi, S., DiLavore, P. S., Shulman, C., Thurm, A., & Pickles, A. (2006). Autism from 2 to 9 years of age. *Archives of General Psychiatry, 63*(6), 694–701.

43. Bailey, J., & Burch, M. (2010). *25 essential skills and strategies for the professional behavior analyst: Expert tips for maximizing consulting effectiveness.* Routledge; Friman, P. C. (2010). Come on in, the water is fine: Achieving mainstream relevance through integration with primary care. *Behavior Analyst, 33,* 19–36.

44. Satcher, D. (2000). Mental health: A report of the Surgeon General—executive summary. *Professional Psychology: Research and Practice, 31*(1), 5–13, 5.

45. Chance, P. (2008). *The teacher's craft: The 10 essential skills of effective teaching.* Waveland; Reed, D. D., Yanagita, B. T., Becirevic, A., Hirst, J. M., Kaplan, B.A., Eastes, E., & Hanna, T. (2016). *Actively caring for higher education.* In E. S. Geller (Ed). *Applied psychology: Actively caring for people* (pp. 563–593). Cambridge University Press.

46. Thorndike, E. L. (1931). *Human learning.* MIT Press.

47. Cialdini, R. B., Eisenberg, N., Green, B. L., Rhoads, K., & Bator, R. (1998). Undermining the undermining effect of reward in sustained interest: When unnecessary conditions are sufficient. *Journal of Applied Social Psychology, 28*(3), 249–263; Kraut, R. E. (1973). Effects of social labeling on giving to charity. *Journal of Experimental Social Psychology, 9*(6), 551–562. Tybout, A. M., & Yalch, R. F. (1980). The effect of experience: A matter of salience? *Journal of Consumer Research, 6*(4), 406–413.

48. Watson, D. L., & Tharp, R. G. (2002). *Self-directed behavior: Self-modification for personal adjustment* (8th ed). Thompson Learning, Inc.

49. Geller, E.S., Bruff, C. D., & Nimmer, J. G. (1985). The "flash for life": A community prompting strategy for safety-belt promotion. *Journal of Applied Behavior Analysis, 18*(4), 145–159.

50. Geller, E. S., Hickmen, J. S., & Pettinger, C. B. (2004). The airline lifesaver: A 17-year analysis of a technique to prompt safety-belt use. *Journal of Safety Research, 35*(4), 357–366.

51. Alderson-Day, B., & Fernyhough, C. (2015). Inner speech: Development, cognitive functions, phenomenology, and neurobiology. *Psychological Bulletin, 141*(5), 931–965.

52. Flammer, A. (1995). Developmental analysis of control beliefs. In A. Bandura (Ed.), *Self-efficacy in changing societies.* Cambridge University Press.

53. James, W. (1890/1981). *The principles of psychology.* Harvard University Press, 313.

54. Carnegie, D. (1936). *How to win friends and influence people* (1981 ed.). Simon & Schuster, 19.

55. Leung, A. K. C., Marchland, V., & Suave, R. S. (2012). The "picky eater": The toddler or preschooler who does not eat. *Pediatric Child Health, 17*(8), 455–457.

56. Michael, J. (1982). Distinguishing between discriminative and motivational functions of stimuli. *Journal of the Experimental Analysis of Behavior, 37*(1), 149–155.

57. Meltzer, L. J., & Mindell, J. A. (2007). Relationship between child sleep disturbances and maternal sleep, mood, and parenting stress: A pilot study. *Journal of Family Psychology, 21*(1), 67–73.

58. Owens, J. A. (2005). Epidemiology of sleep disorders during childhood. In S. H. Sheldon, R. Ferber, & M. H. Kryger (Eds.). *Principles and practices of pediatric sleep medicine* (pp. 27–33). Elsevier Saunders.

59. Adair, R. H., & Bauchner, H. (1993). Sleep problems in childhood. *Current Problems in Pediatrics, 23,* 147–170; Moor, T., & Ucko, C. (1957). Night waking in early infancy: Part I. *Archives of Disease in Children, 32*(164), 333–342.

60. American Sleep Association. (n.d.). *Children and sleep.* http://www.sleepassociation.org/patients-general-public/children-and-sleep/

61. Thiedke, C. C. (2001). Sleep disorders and sleep problems in childhood. *American Family Physician, 63*(2), 277–284.

62. Mindell, J. A., Meltzer, L. J., Carskadon, M. A., & Chervin, R. D. (2009). Developmental aspects of sleep hygiene: Findings from the 2004 National Sleep Foundation sleep in America poll. *Sleep Medicine, 10*(7), 771–779.

63. Ferber, R. (1985). *Solve your child's sleep problems.* Simon & Schuster.

64. Mindell, J. A., Huhn, B., Lewin, D. S., Meltzer, L. J., & Sadeh, A. (2006). Behavioral treatment of bedtime problems and night wakings in infants and young children. *Pediatric Sleep, 29*(10), 1263–1276, 1263.

65. Hauri, P. (1977). *Current concepts: The sleep disorders.* Upjohn.

66. Lacks, P., & Rotert, M. (1986). Knowledge and practice of sleep hygiene techniques in insomniacs and good sleepers. *Behavior Research & Therapy, 24*(3), 365–368.

67. Azrin, N. H., & Foxx, R. M. (1989). *Toilet training in less than a day.* Pocket Books.

68. Gorski, P. A. (1999). Toilet training guidelines: Parents—the role of parents in toilet training. *Pediatrics, 103,* 362–363.

69. Azrin, N. H., & Foxx, R. M. (1973). Dry pants: A rapid method of toilet training children. *Behavior Research and Therapy, 11*(4), 435–442; Kaerts, N., Van Hal, G., Vermandel, A., & Wyndaele, J. J. (2012). Readiness signs used to define the proper moment to start toilet training: A review of the literature. *Neurourology and Urodynamics, 31*(4), 437–440.

70. *Merriam-Webster Dictionary.* (1989). Merriam Webster, Inc., 527.

71. Ibid., *248.*

72. *American Heritage Dictionary.* (1985). (2nd college ed). Houghton Mifflin Company. 449.

73. Ibid., 1231.

74. Covey, S. R. (1989). *The seven habits of highly effective people.* Simon & Schuster, 236–260.

75. Watson, P. C. (1960). On the failure to eliminate hypotheses in a conceptual task. *Quarterly Journal of Experimental Psychology, 12*(3), 129–140; Watson, P. C. (1981). The importance of cognitive illusions. *Behavioral and Brain Sciences, 4*(3), 317–370.

76. Langer, E. (1989). *Mindfulness.* Addison-Wesley.

77. Deci, E. L., & Flaste, R. (1995). *Why we do what we do: Understanding self-motivation.* Penguin; Geller, E. S. (2016). The psychology of self-motivation. In E. S. Geller. (Ed.). *Applied psychology: Actively caring for people* (pp. 83–118). Cambridge University Press; Geller, E. S., & Veazie, R. A. (2017). *The motivation to actively care: How you can make it happen.* Morgan James.

78. White, R. W. (1959). Motivation reconsidered: The concept of competence. *Psychological Review, 66*(5), 297–321.

79. Deci, E. L., & Flaste, R. (1995). *Why we do what we do: Understanding self-motivation.* Penguin. 66.

80. Chance, P. (2008). *The teacher's craft: The 10 essential skills of effective teaching.* Waveland. 95.

81. Geller, E. S. (1996). *The psychology of safety: How to improve behaviors and attitudes on the job.* Chilton Book Company; Geller, E. S. (1998). *Understanding behavior-based safety: Step-by-step methods to improve your workplace* (2nd ed.). J. J. Keller & Associates, Inc.; Geller, E. S. (2001). *The psychology of safety handbook.* CRC Press; Geller, E. S. (2005). *People-based safety: The source.* Coastal Training and Technologies Corporation; Geller, E. S., & Geller, K. S. (2017). *Actively caring for people's safety: How to cultivate a brother's/sister's keeper work culture.* American Society of Safety Professionals; Krause, T. R., Hidley, J. H., & Hodson, S. J. (1996). *The behavior-based safety process: Managing improvement for an injury-free culture* (2nd ed.). Van Nostrand Reinhold; McSween, T. E. (2003). The values-based safety process: Improving your safety culture with a behavioral approach (2nd ed.). Van Nostrand Reinhold.

82. Deci, E. L., & Flaste, R. (1995). *Why we do what we do: Understanding self-motivation.* Penguin. 88.

83. Geller, E. S., & Veazie, B. (2017). *The motivation to actively care: How you can make it happen.* Morgan James.

84. Geller, E. S. (1994). Ten principles for achieving a total safety culture. *Professional Safety, 39*(9), 18–25; Geller, E. S. (2001). *The psychology of safety handbook.* CRC Press; Geller, E. S. (2005). *People-based safety: The source.* Coastal Training Technologies Corp.

85. Block, P. (2008). *Community: The structure of belonging.* Berrett-Koehler.

86. Peck, M. S. (1979). *The different drum: Community making and peace.* Simon & Schuster.

87. Deming, W. E. (1986). *Out of the crisis.* Massachusetts Institute of Technology, Center for Advanced Engineering Study; Deming, W. E. (1993). *The new economics for industry, government, education.* Massachusetts Institute of Technology, Center for Advanced Engineering Study.

88. Senge, P. M. (1990). *The fifth discipline: The art and practice of the learning organization.* Doubleday.

89. Covey, S. R. (1989). *The seven habits of highly effective people.* Simon & Schuster, Inc.

90. Geller, E. S., & Veazie, B. (2017). *The courage to actively care: How to cultivate a culture of interpersonal compassion.* Morgan James.

91. Geller, E. S. (2005). *People-based safety: The source.* Coastal Training Technologies Corp. 95–98.

92. Bandura, A. (1977). *Self-efficacy: The exercise of control.* W. H. Freeman.

93. Maslow, A. H. (1971). *The farther reaches of human nature.* Viking.

94. Colvin, G., Tobin, T., Beard, K., Hagan, S., & Sprague, J. (1998). The school bully: Assessing the problem, developing interventions, and future research directions. *Journal of Behavioral Education, 8*(3), 293–319.

95. Ttofi, M. M., & Farrington, D. P. (2010). Effectiveness of school-based programs to reduce bullying: A systematic and meta-analytical review. *Journal of Experimental Criminology, 7*(1), 27–56.

96. Swearer, S. M., Espelage, D. L., Vaillancourt, T., & Hymel, S. (2010). What can be done about school bullying? Linking research to educational practice. *Educational Researcher, 39*(1), 38–47.

97. Sidman, M. (1989). *Coercion and its fallout.* Authors Cooperative.

98. Miltenberger, R. G. (1997). *Behavior modification: Principles and procedures.* Brooks-Cole; Ogier, R., & Hornby, G. (1996). Effects of differential reinforcement on the behavior and self-esteem of children with emotional and behavioral disorders. *Journal of Behavioral Education, 6*(4), 501–510.

99. Simpson, B., & Willer, R. (2008). Altruism and indirect reciprocity: The interaction of person and situation in prosocial behavior. *Social Psychology Quarterly, 71*(1), 37–52.

100. Honig, A. S., & Pollack, B. (1990). Effects of a brief intervention program to promote prosocial behaviors in young children. *Early Education and Development, 1*(6), 438–444.

101. Demaray, M. K., & Malecki, C. K. (2006). A review of the use of social support in anti-bullying programs. *Journal of School Violence, 5*(3), 51–70.

102. McCarty, S. M., & Geller, E. S. (2011). Want to get rid of bullying? Then reward behavior that is incompatible with it. *Behavior Analysis Digest International, 23*(2), 1–7; McCarty, S. M., Teie, S., McCutchen, J., & Geller, E. S. (2016). Actively caring to prevent bullying in an elementary school: Prompting and rewarding prosocial behavior. *Journal of Prevention & Intervention in the Community, 44*(3), 164–176.

103. Raboteau, A. (2011, July 25). *Psychology professor, students say recognizing daily acts of kindness makes a huge impact.* Virginia Tech: Spotlight. https://www.tandfonline.com/doi/abs/10.1080/10852352.2016.1166809?src=recsys&journalCode=wpic20

104. Cialdini, R. B. (2001). *Influence: Science and practice* (6th ed.). Pearson Education; Furrow, C., & Geller, E. S. (2016). Social influence and AC4P behavior. In E. S. Geller (Ed.). *Applied psychology: Actively caring for people* (pp. 185–227). Cambridge University Press.

105. Krevans, J., & Gibbs, J.C. (2008). Parents' use of inductive discipline: Relations to children's empathy and prosocial behavior. *Child Development, 67*(6), 3263–3277.

106. Festinger, L. (1957). *A theory of cognitive dissonance.* Stanford University Press.

107. Conari Press. (1993). *Random acts of kindness.*

108. Kahneman, D. (2011). *Thinking, fast and slow.* Farrar, Straus & Giroux.

SUGGESTED READINGS

1. Azrin, N. H., & Foxx, R. M. (1989). *Toilet training in less than a day*. Pocket Books.

2. Barkley, R. A. (2013). *Your defiant child: Eight steps to better behavior* (2nd ed.). Guilford.

3. Biglan, A. (2015). *The nurture effect: How the science of human behavior can improve our lives and our world*. New Harbinger.

4. Covey, S. R. (1989). *The seven habits of highly effective people: Restoring the character ethic*. Simon & Schuster.

5. Dweck, C. S. (2006). *Mindset: The new psychology of success*. Ballantine Books.

6. Geller, E. S. (2016) (Ed.). *Applied psychology: Actively caring for people*. Cambridge University Press.

7. Geller, E. S. (2020). *Life lessons from psychological science: Understanding and improving interpersonal dynamics*. Cognella.

8. Geller, E. S., & Veazie, B. (2017). *The motivation to actively care: How you can make it happen*. Morgan James.

9. Holdsambeck, R. D., & Pennypacker, H. S. (2016) (Eds.). *Behavioral science: Tales of inspiration, discovery, and service*. Cambridge Center for Behavioral Studies.

10. Watson, D. L., & Tharp, R. G. (2002). *Self-directed behavior: Self-modification for personal adjustment* (8th ed.). Thompson Learning, Inc.

NAME AND SUBJECT INDEX

ABOUT THE AUTHORS

E. Scott Geller, Ph.D., an alumni distinguished professor at Virginia Tech, is cofounder and senior partner of Safety Performance Solutions, Inc., a leading-edge training and consulting organization specializing in AC4P safety since 1995 (safetyperformance.com). For five decades, Professor Geller has taught and conducted research as a faculty member and director of the Center for Applied Behavior Systems in the Department of Psychology at Virginia Tech (VT).

He has authored, edited, or coauthored 51 books, 94 book chapters, 39 training programs, 259 magazine articles, and more than 300 research articles addressing the development and evaluation of behavior change interventions to improve quality of life on a large scale. His most recent textbook, *Applied Psychology: Actively Caring for People,* defines Dr. Geller's research, teaching, and scholarship career at Virginia Tech, which epitomizes the VT logo: *Ut Prosim*–"That I May Serve."

His popular books in applied psychology include *The Psychology of Safety: Improving Behaviors and Attitudes on the Job; Working Safe; Understanding Behavior-Based Safety; Building Successful Safety Teams; Beyond Safety Accountability: How to Increase Personal Responsibility; The Psychology of Safety Handbook; Keys to Behavior-Based Safety from Safety Performance Solutions; The Participation Factor; People-Based Safety: The Source; People-Based Patient Safety: Enriching Your Culture to Prevent Medical Error,* coauthored with Dave Johnson; *Leading People-Based Safety: Enriching Your Culture; Actively Caring for People: Cultivating a Culture of Compassion; Actively Caring for People in Schools: How to Cultivate a Culture of Compassion; The Courage to Actively Care: Cultivating a Culture of Interpersonal Compassion; and The Motivation to Actively Care: How You Can Make It Happen,* both coauthored with the late Bob Veazie; *Actively Caring for People Policing: Building Positive Police/Citizen Relations,* coauthored by Bobby Kipper; *Fifty Lessons to Enrich Your Life: Proven Principles from Psychological Science,* and *Actively Caring for People's Safety: How to Cultivate a Brother's/Sister's Keeper Culture,* coauthored with his daughter, Krista S. Geller, PhD.

Dr. Geller is a fellow of the American Psychological Society, the Association for Psychological Science, the Association of Behavior Analysis International, and the World Academy of Productivity and Quality Sciences. He is past editor of *Journal of Applied Behavior Analysis* (1989–1992), past associate editor of *Environment and Behavior* (1982–2017), and current consulting editor for *Behavior and Social Issues, Journal of Organizational Behavior Management,* and *Journal of Safety Research.*

Dr. Geller has received lifetime achievement awards from the International Organizational Behavior Management Network (in 2008) and the American Psychological Foundation (in 2009).

In 2010, he was honored with the Outstanding Applied Research award from the American Psychological Association's Division of Applied Behavior Analysis. In 2019, Professor Geller received the APA Division 25 Nathan H. Azrin Distinguished Contributions to Applied Behavior Analysis award. In 2011, the College of Wooster awarded E. Scott Geller the honorary degree: Doctor of Humane Letters.

Angela K. Fournier, Ph.D. is a professor in the Department of Psychology at Bemidji State University, where she teaches undergraduates in psychology and serves as director of the Human-Animal Interaction Laboratory. Dr. Fournier's research and scholarship are in the areas of large-scale intervention to improve community health behavior and the psychological outcomes of animal-assisted interventions. She is author of over 20 peer-reviewed journal articles and book chapters, and she is a licensed clinical psychologist. Dr. Fournier is a certified mental health specialist with the Equine-Assisted Growth and Learning Association and co-facilitates equine-assisted psychotherapy and learning at Eagle Vista Ranch and Wellness Center in Bemidji, Minnesota. Her clinical and academic efforts are aimed at making a beneficial difference in the lives of others, an AC4P passion that was ignited when working with Professor Scott Geller as a graduate student of clinical science in the Center for Applied Behavior Systems in the Department of Psychology at Virginia Tech.

www.ingramcontent.com/pod-product-compliance
Lightning Source LLC
Chambersburg PA
CBHW081436270326
41932CB00019B/3220

* 9 7 8 1 7 9 3 5 1 0 0 1 3 *